CARING
FOR CREATION

Biblical and theological perspectives

CARING FOR CREATION

Biblical and theological perspectives

Edited by SARAH TILLETT

This compilation copyright © A Rocha 2005

Published by
The Bible Reading Fellowship
First Floor, Elsfield Hall
15–17 Elsfield Way, Oxford OX2 8FG
Website: www.brf.org.uk

ISBN 1 84101 439 7
First published 2005
10 9 8 7 6 5 4 3 2 1 0
All rights reserved

Acknowledgments
Unless otherwise stated, scripture quotations are taken from the Holy Bible, New
International Version, copyright © 1973, 1978, 1984 by International Bible Society, and
are used by permission of Hodder & Stoughton Limited. All rights reserved. 'NIV' is a
registered trademark of International Bible Society. UK trademark number 1448790.

Scripture quotations taken from The New Revised Standard Version of the Bible, copyright
© 1946, 1952, 1971 by the Division of Christian Education of the National Council of the
Churches of Christ in the USA, are used by permission. All rights reserved.

Scripture quotations taken from The Revised Standard Version of the Bible, Anglicized
Edition, copyright © 1989, 1995 by the Division of Christian Education of the National
Council of the Churches of Christ in the USA, are used by permission. All rights reserved.

The Holy Bible, English Standard Version, copyright © 2001 by Crossway Bibles, a division
of Good News Publishers.

Extracts from the Authorized Version of the Bible (The King James Bible), the rights in
which are vested in the Crown, are reproduced by permission of the Crown's patentee,
Cambridge University Press.

A catalogue record for this book is available from the British Library

Printed in Singapore by Craft Print International Ltd

CONTENTS

Chapter Ten

Chapter Eleven

Chapter Twelve

CONTRIBUTORS

Dr Vijay D. Anand worked at the Asian Elephant Research and Conservation Centre in Bangalore, and completed a PhD in human/wildlife land use issues, before becoming National Director of A Rocha India: india@arocha.org

Dr R.J. Berry is a member of the A Rocha International Council of Reference. He was Professor of Genetics at University College, London from 1978 to 2000, and a former President of the Linnean Society, the British Ecological Society, the European Ecological Federation, and of Christians in Science. He is Moderator of the Environmental Issues Network of Churches Together in Britain and Ireland. Among other publications, he has written *God and Evolution* (Hodder & Stoughton, 1988), *God and the Biologist* (IVP, 1996), *Science, Life and Christian Belief* (with Malcolm Jeeves) (IVP, 1998), *God's Book of Works* (T&T Clark, 2003), and is editor of *Real Science, Real Faith* (Monarch, 1991), *Environmental Dilemmas* (Chapman & Hall, 1993), and *The Care of Creation* (IVP, 2000).

Mrs Karin Boisclair-Joly and her husband Alain are wardens of A Rocha France's residential field studies centre in Provence, as well as bringing up a young family. The centre welcomes volunteers and visitors: france@arocha.org

The Revd Dave Bookless is Director of A Rocha UK, based in Southall, London, where 'A Rocha Living Waterways'—the first UK project—is located. Ordained in the Church of England in 1991, he moved to Southall, where he was a curate in one church, then priest-in-charge of another. He has always had a love for the natural world—training as a bird-ringer—and got involved with A Rocha from 1994, becoming a Trustee in 1996. At the start of 2001, Dave and his wife Anne became co-founders of A Rocha UK (uk@arocha.org), and team leaders for the 'A Rocha Living Waterways' project, seeking to create a 'greener, cleaner Southall and Hayes'.

Dr Peter Carruthers is a director of the John Ray Initiative (JRI), an educational charity that aims to develop and communicate a Christian understanding of the environment. An agricultural scientist, he worked for many years at Reading University, combining research in the Centre for Agricultural Strategy and lecturing in Agricultural Systems. He is Chairman of the Agricultural Christian Fellowship, a Trustee/Director of Farm Crisis Network, a Member of the Institute of Biology and a Chartered Biologist, and now works for the Countryside Agency.

Mr Marcial Felgueiras is Director of A Rocha Portugal, and lives at the first A Rocha centre, Cruzinha, with his wife Paula and their children. The centre welcomes volunteers and guests: portugal@arocha.org

Mrs Miranda Harris moved to southern Portugal in 1983 with her husband Peter, and founded A Rocha. She is now Pastoral Director of A Rocha International and, in shaping the vision and ethos of the organization, draws on her experience of welcoming visitors from all over the world to the Portuguese centre. She and Peter now travel extensively as they oversee new A Rocha projects around the world, but they still enjoy welcoming visitors to their home near the A Rocha France centre.

The Revd Peter Harris worked with his wife Miranda in Portugal from 1983 to 1995, running A Rocha's first field study centre and bird observatory near Lagos. Since 1987, they have been living in France, working with national colleagues to establish and run a similar centre, while coordinating A Rocha projects now active in 14 other countries around the world. They have experience of mission projects in Asia, Africa, the Middle East and South America, and have served as adjunct faculty members of Regent College, Vancouver. Their story is told in *Under the Bright Wings* (Hodder & Stoughton, 1993). Peter has contributed to *The Lion Handbook of World Christianity* (Lion, 1989), *The Care of Creation*, edited by R.J. Berry (IVP, 2000), *God's Stewards: The Role of Christians in Creation Care*, edited by Don Brandt (World Vision, 2002), and *Down-to-Earth Christianity*, edited by W. Dayton Roberts (AERDO, 2000).

Sir John Houghton has been chairman of the John Ray Initiative since it was founded in 1997. He has held positions as Professor of Atmospheric Physics at Oxford University (1976–83), Director General and Chief Executive of the UK Meteorological Office (1983–91), Chairman of the UK Royal Commission on Environmental Pollution (1992–98), chairman or co-chairman of the Scientific Assessment for the Intergovernmental Panel on Climate Change (1988–2002), member of the UK Government Panel on Sustainable Development (1994–2000). He has written a number of books, including *The Physics of Atmospheres* (3rd edn, Cambridge University Press, 2002), *Global Warming: the Complete Briefing* (3rd edn, Cambridge University Press, 2004) and *The Search for God: Can Science Help?* (Lion, 1995).

Dr James Houston is a specialist in historical geography, teaching for 23 years at Oxford University, where he was a Fellow of Hertford College. He was founding Principal and Chancellor of Regent College, Vancouver, where he taught as Professor of Spiritual Theology until his retirement in 2000. Author and editor of over 35 books, he wrote *I Believe in the Creator* (Eerdmans, 1978).

Mrs Leah Kostamo shares leadership of A Rocha Canada with her husband Markku, as well as bringing up a young family. They live at the A Rocha Canada centre, which is a ten-acre site south of Vancouver, with a salmon stream. The centre opened in 2003 and welcomes visitors: canada@arocha.org

Mr Chris Magero has a degree in Range (Wildlife) Management and spent a year volunteering with A Rocha UK before returning to Kenya. A Rocha Kenya's centre, Mwamba, welcomes volunteers and visitors: kenya@arocha.org

Mr Chris Naylor is a geography teacher by training, and is founder director of A Rocha Lebanon. Chris lives in Beirut with his wife Susanna and three children, and oversees A Rocha's work in the Aammiq Marsh: lebanon@arocha.org

Eugene H. Peterson is a pastor, scholar, writer and poet. He has written more than 20 books, including *A Long Obedience in the Same Direction* (IVP, 1980), *The Contemplative Pastor* (Word Books, 1989) and *Leap Over a Wall* (HarperCollins, 1997). He is Professor Emeritus of Spiritual Theology at Regent College in Vancouver, Canada, and also founded Christ Our King Presbyterian Church in Bel Air, Maryland, where he was the pastor for 29 years.

Sir Ghillean T. Prance was Director of the Royal Botanic Gardens, Kew, 1988–99, having previously worked at the New York Botanical Gardens. He is currently Scientific Director of the Eden Project, Cornwall. He has undertaken numerous botanical expeditions to Amazonia, a topic on which he has published widely. Among his recent publications is *The Earth under Threat: a Christian Perspective* (Wild Goose Publications, 1996). He is a visiting professor at Reading University, and a past president of the Linnean Society and the Institute of Biology. He is a fellow of the Royal Geographical Society, the American Association for the Advancement of Science, and the Royal Society, and was knighted in 1995.

Dr Vinoth Ramachandra lives in Colombo, Sri Lanka. He holds degrees in nuclear engineering from London University and works with the International Fellowship of Evangelical Students (IFES) as the Secretary for Dialogue and Social Engagement (Asia). His most recent book is *The Message of Mission* (2003; co-authored with Howard Peskett) in the IVP *Bible Speaks Today* series.

Mr Will Simonson left a key post at English Nature to become A Rocha International's Scientific Co-coordinator. With his wife Rachel and their children, they are based at A Rocha Portugal: simonsons@arocha.org

The Revd Pavel Svetlik is founder of A Rocha Czech Republic, an ordained minister of the Czech Brethren, and one of the most experienced bird-ringers in Eastern Europe. A Rocha Czech's new centre is due to open for visitors late in 2005: czech@arocha.org

The Revd Sarah Tillett was ordained in the Church of England in 2003 and is curate at Knowle parish church in the West Midlands. She has a Masters in Christian Studies from Regent College, Vancouver, Canada. Before entering ordained ministry she was a broadcaster and writer and lived in Hong Kong. Sarah is a Trustee and director of Tearfund UK, Chaplain to the Church of England's Media Council and a supporter of A Rocha International.

Ms Ginny Vroblesky has been involved with Christian environmental concerns for many years, most recently becoming A Rocha USA's first staff member, based near Washington DC: usa@arocha.org

11

Dr Christopher J.H. Wright is one of the most significant writers on Old Testament Ethics and is International Ministries Director of the Langham Partnership International. He was formerly Principal of All Nations Christian College and taught at Union Biblical Seminary, Pune, India. He has written several books, including *The Uniqueness of Jesus* (2001, Monarch), the New International Biblical Commentary on *Deuteronomy* (Paternoster, 1996), *The Message of Ezekiel* (IVP, 2001) and *Old Testament Ethics for the People of God* (IVP, 2004).

FOREWORD

At least in evangelical circles, creation is a much-neglected biblical topic and caring for creation an equally neglected responsibility.

So I am delighted with this symposium. Here is a team of distinguished Christian leaders, representing a variety of different disciplines, who lay down solid theological foundations for our Christian environment stewardship and call us to involvement in restoring threatened and damaged habitats.

One of the most encouraging developments during the last quarter of the 20th century was the emergence of Christian environmental groups, which have discovered something of the planet's rich biodiversity and are determined to play their part in preserving it. Among them is A Rocha, sub-titled 'Christians in Conservation', which is spreading worldwide almost spontaneously.

We are now faced with the crisis of climate change. My hope and prayer are that Christians will be found in the vanguard of those who influence public opinion and agitate for governmental action. To that end, this book should make a significant contribution.

John Stott

INTRODUCTION

The destruction of habitats in many countries around the world is one of the main causes for the current loss of a wide variety of plant and animal species in their natural environment (biodiversity). The decline of biodiversity can be rapid and dramatic or very slow. Either way, the consequences of the loss of biodiversity affect the capacity of the land to sustain human needs and diminish the world's wealth of plants and animals.

In the Bible, God creates men and women in his own image and asks us to reflect his image in our stewardship over 'the fish of the sea and the birds of the air, over the livestock, over all the earth, and over all the creatures that move along the ground' (Genesis 1:26). The image we reflect should be one of unselfish love, mercy, tender compassion and justice. Unfortunately, our rebellious human nature makes us selfish, and our concern for the world we live in is often characterized by cruelty, greed and short-sightedness rather than love and compassion. The environment is an issue of justice, and when the environment is damaged it is often the poor who suffer the most.

In a global context it is easy to be overwhelmed by the problems of the destruction of the environment: deforestation, disintegration of coral reefs, the extinction of species, over-fishing, global warming and a multitude of other disasters and gloomy forecasts can cause us to wonder if our pitiful action will really make any difference. But the Bible clearly shows us that there are grounds for hope. Both Isaiah and Hosea prophesy about a time to come when there will be human and environmental harmony. In the New Testament Jesus is described as the Saviour of fallen humanity, and also the one for whom all creation was made and through whom all creation will one day be liberated from its bondage to decay.

Many ecologists, environmentalists and economists hold the view that religion has been the primary cause of ecological crisis and that it has little to offer in the robust scientific debates surrounding issues such as global warming and species extinction. It has also been suggested that anti-intellectualism in the Church has blocked the way for any Christian influence in scientific debates. Mark Noll argues in his book *The Scandal of the Evangelical Mind* that early evangelicalism abandoned the academy to the enlightened scientists and lost its credibility as an influence in our Western cultures, only to focus on conversionism, biblicism and activism. He claimed that Christians were living on the periphery of responsible intellectual existence: 'To be spiritual one must no longer pay attention to the world.'[1] Care for the world has been seen as some loony green association with the environmental movement. Ronald Sider, a principal sponsor of the Evangelical Declaration on the Care of Creation,[2] proposes that the science of modern environmentalism and the spiritual quest it represents can only be fulfilled through using biblical truth as the foundation for working seriously at our environmental problems.

This book brings together some of the main biblical themes of creation, fall, redemption and resurrection, the way that they relate to God's concern for his creation and the God-given human responsibility to care for, preserve and develop his Earth on his behalf. It aims to address some of the misconceptions and misinterpretations of many Christians and ecologists regarding the care of creation, and it aims to create awareness of the possibilities for combining rigorous but wise use of science and technology with responsible environmental stewardship in accordance with Christian principles. Stories from the A Rocha centres around the world illustrate how technical scientific knowledge and a biblical ethos are brought together to develop sustainable communities, demonstrating good environmental stewardship and encouraging others to similar action.

Environmental issues are a growing concern for many people, religious and non-religious alike. This book offers a biblical, theological and spiritual springboard from which we can launch discussions and debate and explore opportunities for growth and awareness as responsible stewards of God's creation. Eugene Peterson challenges us to read Genesis 1 with a new perspective, not just as the story of how things began but as a way to live today. This, says Peterson, means 'keeping creation time' as though it were a gift from God. The new perspective on time 'erects a bastion in time against the commodification of time, reducing time to money or what we can get out of it'. A Rocha Canada's story illustrates the keeping of creation time in the life cycles of the Pacific salmon, whose instinctive bell rings, telling it to return home to the stream where it was spawned in order to spawn and then die.

Physicist John Houghton argues from scripture that true science and true religion do indeed go hand in hand and illuminate each other. On the ground, though, the light has not yet dawned, as A Rocha India grapples with the conflict between the Indian elephant and local communities in Bannerghatta National Park.

Biblically, the root of all the environmental problems lies at the feet of fallen humanity and our rejection of the creator. Sam Berry explores a way of understanding the story of fallen humanity against the background of the 21st century. Peter Harris suggests a re-reading of God's covenant with Noah that is less anthropocentric and that incorporates the whole of God's creation, opening a door to the redemption of all that God has made.

Chris Wright points to a way of ethical living that is deeply embedded in Old Testament scriptures and jubilee laws. The sense of hopelessness we feel about effecting change in our world is in some ways appropriate if we are to understand the limitations of humanity in a proper relationship to God. James Houston considers the development of theological thinking and the cultural influences that have led to human independence from God. Most theologians recognize that there is an eschatological purpose in creation and Houston highlights the significance of the Sabbath in understanding the consummation of God's work of creation and his purposes in redemption. He says that Sabbath rest is a reminder that 'I am confident of this, that the one who began a good work among you will bring it to completion by the day of Jesus Christ' (Philippians 1:6, NRSV).

We do not know how the redemption of creation will take place. We do know that we have a part to play and a God-given responsibility towards all that God has made. Therefore we can be sure that God, who created and sustains his world, wants all his people to be actively involved in his plan to redeem the whole of creation. So our hope is in the words of Revelation 21:1–5:

Then I saw a new heaven and a new earth, for the first heaven and the first earth had passed away, and there was no longer any sea. I saw the Holy City, the new Jerusalem, coming down out of heaven from God, prepared as a bride beautifully dressed for her husband. And I heard a loud voice from the throne saying, 'Now the dwelling of God is with men, and he will live with them. They will be his people, and God himself will be with them and be their God. He will wipe every tear from their eyes. There will be no more death or mourning or crying or pain, for the old order of things has passed away.' He who was seated on the throne said, 'I am making everything new!' Then he said, 'Write this down, for these words are trustworthy and true.'

A ROCHA

A Rocha is an international Christian organization dedicated to environmental conservation, and a registered charity. It was launched in Portugal in 1983 and focuses primarily on community-based projects. *A Rocha* is Portuguese and means 'The Rock'. The name has a threefold significance for the organization: firstly it is taken from the name of the headland in Portugal where the first project was established, *Quinta da Rocha*; secondly it indicates the solid basis of scientific studies practised through A Rocha's various centres; and finally, 'the rock' is a biblical description of the nature of God and affirms A Rocha's Christian distinctiveness.

A Rocha currently works in 15 countries, across five continents, including the UK. It is also a member of IUCN (the International Conservation Union). The work of A Rocha across the world is identified by the practical outworking of five core commitments:

- **Christian:** Underlying all it does is biblical faith in the living God, who made the world, loves it and entrusts it to the care of human society.
- **Conservation:** A Rocha carries out research for the conservation and restoration of the natural world and runs environmental education programmes for people of all ages.
- **Community:** Through commitment to God, fellow human beings and the wider creation, A Rocha aims to develop good relationships both within the A Rocha 'family' and in local communities where the charity works.
- **Cross-cultural:** It draws on the insights and skills of people from diverse cultures, both locally and around the world.
- **Cooperation:** It works in partnership with a wide variety of organizations and individuals who share A Rocha's concern for a sustainable world.

A Rocha UK was founded in 2001 by the Revd Dave Bookless and his wife Anne. The organization is interdenominational and a member of the Evangelical Alliance. It has a long-term vision with the following objectives:

- To learn from and share with A Rocha's international family of projects, encouraging and supporting conservation work around the world.

- To create a network of Christ-centred, community-based, practical conservation projects throughout the UK.
- To encourage the Church to understand the biblical responsibility to act as good stewards of God's world, and to provide practical advice on how to go about this.
- To advocate and resource action locally, nationally and internationally, in pursuit of environmental protection and sustainable development.
- To produce educational material for schools and churches, including material to celebrate Environment Sunday (formerly Conservation Sunday) on the Sunday closest to World Environment Day (5 June).
- To offer advice to Christian landowners, organizations and farmers on a biblical and practical approach to stewardship of the earth.

A Rocha UK's first project is 'Living Waterways', a community-centred project based in multi-cultural Southall and Hayes, London. The project has led to the restoration of 90 acres of derelict land into the Minet Country Park and nature area—the result of a successful campaign with local landowners, Hillingdon Council and other community groups. The park has wildlife conservation areas, open recreational space and a children's playground; it was formerly home to burnt-out cars, fly-tipped waste and illegal motorbike scrambling. It has been shortlisted for the London Planning Awards (for partnership with a local authority) and the 'Faithworks' awards for faith-inspired community projects (administered by the Oasis Trust and Spring Harvest). A Rocha UK has a community house and field study centre in Southall, where the UK team of twelve are based and volunteers can stay.

A Rocha UK is a registered charity with a council of reference that includes the Rt Revd James Jones, Sir John Houghton, Sir Ghillean Prance, Ram Gidoomal CBE, the Revd Dr Rob Frost, the Revd Steve Chalke, Dr Elaine Storkey and Professor Graham Ashworth.

A Rocha UK, 13 Avenue Road, Southall, Middlesex UB1 3BL
Tel: 020 8574 5935
E-mail: uk@arocha.org
Website: www.arocha.org

CREATION AND THE GIFT OF TIME

Eugene Peterson

The Holy Spirit has descended on this old world of ours. Psalm 29 asks us to worship the Lord in the beauty of holiness. We look around and there it is: a grace revealing gesture, fresh snowfall, a friend's forgiveness, the first migrating yellow warbler, a miracle conversion, a truth-telling poem, pasque-flower in bloom, the good death of a parent, resurrection, Father Son and Holy Spirit, all the endless permutations of life—the beauty of holiness—and we have ringside seats. O worship the Lord in the beauty of holiness.

EUGENE PETERSON, SEATTLE 2001

The two creation stories, Genesis 1 and Genesis 2, set at the entrance to our Bibles, are primarily texts for living in the time and the place that we wake up to each morning.

Each has been studied meticulously by both Jewish and Christian scholars for a couple of thousand years, and their accumulated insights and truths stagger our imaginations. There is so much here to consider and ponder, to appreciate and respond to. What is sometimes missed in this cascade of exegetical brilliance, pouring out of the work of scholars of Genesis 1 and 2, is how skilfully and well these texts lead us ordinary working Christians into the land of the living.

It is easy to miss the personal immediacy of Genesis 1 and 2, as we are sometimes distracted by the polemical debates that involve the big cosmological questions about how things began, or are tempted to use the texts to pick fights with atheists. For a time I was caught up in both of these distractions but also intoxicated with the words, images and syntax, comparing and evaluating these creation stories and contrasting the worlds in ancient Babylonian and Egyptian civilizations.

The challenge in Genesis is to shift from understanding the text as the beginning of all things to listening to the text as a way to begin to live now. When I became a pastor, I gradually realized what powerful texts these are for dealing with life just as we live it day after day. As a pastor, the focus of my life has been to pray and preach and teach the holy scriptures into the lives of everyday people: husbands and wives raising children, engineers building bridges, farmers in the wheat fields and arthritic 80-year-olds in nursing homes. In the course of doing that, I came to think of Genesis 1 and 2 as among the most uninterpreted and under-used texts for shaping an obedient and reverent life, following Jesus in our daily working and worshipping lives.

A PEOPLE IN EXILE

First, I was struck by how the cultural and spiritual conditions in which we are living matched the conditions of the Hebrew people of God in the sixth century BC, a century of exile. The pervasive uprootedness, loss of biblical tradition, lack of moral consensus and common memories, and living far removed from where we grew up, have left people with little sense of place or grounding. These are exile conditions. That is when I discovered the exile texts of Isaiah, pastoral messages to people who have lost touch with their time and place in the world. One of the most important words used by the prophet Isaiah is 'create'. In the Bible it is used exclusively with God as the subject: men and women don't create— God does. When nothing we do makes any difference and we are left standing around clueless, then we are ready for God to create. When the conditions in which we live seem totally alien to life and salvation, we are reduced to waiting for what God can do. The verb 'to create' and the noun 'creator' appear more times in the exilic preaching of Isaiah than in any other place in the Bible (17 times in Isaiah compared to six times in Genesis 1).

In Isaiah, the immediate, powerful, convincing and life-changing creation work of God is among people who feel uncreated, unformed, unfitted for the world in which they find themselves. Under Isaiah's prophetic influence, 'create' emerges from the background of Israel's history into an actively gospel word for what God is doing today around the exile people of today (Isaiah 61).

THE GIFT OF TIME

When we read Genesis from this shifted perspective, we have to ask the question, how can I obey this and live within the gift of God's creation? Genesis 1 presents the gift of creation as the gift of time (Genesis 2 presents the gift of place). The understanding and honouring of time is fundamental to the realization of how we are and how we live. Violations of sacred time become desecrations of our most intimate relations with God and one another. Hours and days, weeks and months and years, these are the stuff of holiness.

One of the many desecrations visited on the creation, the profanation of time ranks near the top. Time is the medium in which we do all our living. When time is desecrated, life is desecrated. Evidence of this desecration is identified through hurry and procrastination. Both violate the sacredness of time. Hurry turns away from the gift of time in a compulsive grasping for abstractions that are not immediately there, but that it can possess and control. Procrastination is distracted from the gift of time in a lazy inattentiveness to the life of obedience and adoration by which we enter into what the apostle Paul called the fullness of time (Galatians 4:4). Genesis 1 is not in a hurry and does not procrastinate.

One of the greatest hindrances to our understanding of the creation gift of time has been a distracted focus and overemphasis on end-times, particularly for those caught up in waiting for the rapture. Ordinary time is not what biblical people endure or put up with until the end-time; it is a gift. End-time influences present time by charging it and filling it with purpose and significance. It is not a future we wait for, but the fullness of time flowing into the present that we receive and live in, in adoration and obedience.

In order to understand the creation gift of time, we must look at the structure of Genesis. The first creation account is arranged in a seven-day sequence. Six times the creation work is introduced with 'And God said'. Six times the segment is concluded with the phrase 'there was evening, and there was morning'. The seventh day is treated differently, which sets it apart for special emphasis and attention. For example, instead of the number being in the concluding phrase of the segment, it is introductory: 'on the seventh day' (2:2). The number seven is repeated twice more in successive sentences: 'By the seventh day God had finished the work he had been doing'; 'so on the seventh day he rested from all his work'; 'And

God blessed the seventh day and made it holy, because on it he rested from all the work of creating that he had done' (2:2–3).

The emphasis is quite different from the rhythm set up in the first six days. God's work of creation is conveyed to us rhythmically: one-two-three / four-five-six / seven-seven-seven (1-2-3 / 4-5-6 / 7-7-7). There are two sets of three days each of creation activity. In the first set of three (1-2-3), the pre-creation chaos mentioned in Genesis 1:2 is *formed*. In the second set of three (4-5-6), the pre-creation emptiness is *filled*. These two sets of creation work, forming and filling, are followed by seventh-day rest in triple emphasis. The third day of each three-day sequence is set apart by having two creation acts, setting up a cadence of one-two-three/three, one-two-three/three, seven/seven/seven. Genesis 1 is a skilfully and rhythmically arranged set of words.

In the past, the text would have been read aloud, enabling the listener to hear and enter into the rhythms of time, internalizing and assimilating the rhythms like a piece of music, 'keeping time'. Old Testament scholar Bruce Waltke calls this the libretto for all of Israel's life. Think of Genesis 1 as an opera and oratorio, expressing the creation rhythms in our language and our work: we are created to live rhythmically.

The seven days of creation are repeated in a sequence of 28 days as the moon circles the earth, and this lunar rhythm is then repeated twelve times. These large rhythms bring us spring birth, summer growth, autumn harvest and winter sleep. Time is rhythmic; we are immersed in rhythms. Life is rhythmic. We ourselves are created rhythmically. We have a pulse that beats; our breath is rhythmic. Our bodies function in cycles of metabolic rhythms. You can speed up or slow down rhythm but you cannot eliminate it. We can disrupt the rhythms, but when we do, we are not living in the created way of our bodies.

The rhythms of time are resolved into the seventh pause—rest, a not doing. The structure of the segments is changed totally. The great Semitic scholar Umberto Cassuto pointed out that each of the sentences in the paragraph in which 'seven' is introduced (Genesis 2:2–3) has seven words, and the seven-day paragraph has 35 words, a multiple of seven. Genesis 1 points to the seventh day as the clue to the meaning of creation. If we are going to live out the theology of creation, we must be personally involved with the seventh day, the Sabbath. Our involvement is made explicit in the Sinai command to keep the Sabbath holy. In the Ten Commandments, the Sabbath is the only creation action that gets attached to a commandment. This means that God's sabbatical rest is something in which we can participate. We can participate in God's creation work. Sabbath is our point of entry into creation.

The scholar Jon Levenson stresses that Genesis 1 accentuates the possibility of human access to the creation rhythms themselves. If Genesis 1 is the text for our understanding and participation in creation, then the Sabbath is the point of entry. The Sinai command is given in two forms, one in Exodus and the other in Deuteronomy. The commands are almost identical in the two listings except for the supporting reason, which is different. The Exodus text says:

Remember the Sabbath day by keeping it holy. Six days you shall labour and do all your work, but the seventh day is a Sabbath to the Lord your God. On it you shall not do any work… **For in six days the Lord made the heavens and the earth, the sea, and all that is in them, but he rested on the seventh day. Therefore the Lord blessed the Sabbath day and made it holy.**
EXODUS 20:8–11

The Deuteronomy text says:

Observe the Sabbath day by keeping it holy, as the Lord your God has commanded you. Six days you shall labour and do all your work, but the seventh day is the Sabbath to the Lord your God. On it you shall not do any work… **Remember that you were slaves in Egypt and that the Lord your God brought you out of there with a mighty hand and an outstretched arm. Therefore the Lord your God has commanded you to observe the Sabbath day.**
DEUTERONOMY 5:12–15

The Exodus command is endorsed by the precedence of God, who rested on the seventh day. When we remember the Sabbath and rest on it, we enter into and participate in and maintain the rhythm of creation, and keep time with God. The Deuteronomy command is endorsed by a sense of social justice. When we remember the Sabbath and rest on it, we enter into and participate in the freedom of creation, the freedom to experience and share God's deliverance.

Keeping creation time preserves time as God's gift of holy rest; it erects a bastion in time against the commodification of time, reducing time to money or what we can get out of it, and having no time for beauty or anything that cannot be purchased or used. The Sabbath command is a defence against the hurry that desecrates time. It preserves and honours time as God's gift of holy freedom. It erects a weekly bastion against the lethargic procrastination that breeds oppression, that lets injustice flourish because we are not attending in obedience and adoration to people and animals and our environment.

CREATION CONTEMPLATION

The Genesis creation days are resolved in an act of rest. The word 'rest' expands and deepens for us if we use a more complex word: 'contemplation'. Contemplation is the practice of assimilating what is given to us and receiving it into our minds and spirits. There is nothing passive or withdrawn about contemplation. It is highly active, deeply energetic; it is neither hurried nor lazy. It requires being present to another, the Other, so that what we cannot do can be done to us through God's creation and the completion of his creation.

Worship is an extension of contemplation. How do we get in touch with God and live more or less in step with God? The obvious answer might be to watch the salmon run or to get a pair of binoculars and take up bird-watching, and become familiar with the colourful ways of hawks and warblers. Or we could get a fly-rod, learn to read the rivers, study which insects are fancied by the fish, and learn how to cast a line lightly on to the waters that are home to brown trout. But the obvious answer is not the right answer. The best thing we can do is to enter a church and worship God. There is ancient and widespread evidence that connects world-making (that is, creation) with temple building (that is, worship) or church building (which serves worship). There is also evidence around the world that connects the ordering of worship and the creation of the world. The point of church building is to realize and extend creation through human enactment, through praise and prayer and by rehearsing and embracing the commandments, promises and blessings of God and putting them into action in the world that we live in. Architecturally, it is to give some symbolic hint and connection between what we are doing in the church and outside the church.

The way in which this Genesis text and the creation gift of time get inside us is through the act of worship. Worship is the primary means in which we become participants in God's work, but if we are not in touch with the way he works, things are diminished considerably. The Genesis work rhythms are brought into focus in the Sabbath rest commands and are reproduced in our lives in the act of worship in a way that enables us to participate. Then, when we walk out of the place of worship, we walk out with fresh recognizing eyes, with a recreated obedient heart into the world in which we are God's image, participating in God's work. Everything we see, feel, touch and taste carries within it the rhythms of 'and God said, "Let there be"'... 'and it was so'... 'and it was good'. We are more deeply in and at home in the creation than ever.

There is a story in Exodus that illustrates this clearly. In Exodus 31—40, Moses goes up on the mountain to receive the Commandments. The story begins and ends with God's command for the people of Israel to observe the Sabbath (Exodus 31:12–18; 35:1–3). The people of Israel are left waiting at the bottom of the mountain, and they get impatient because they don't know how to deal with time. They are in a hurry to get their hands on something, and so they make a golden calf and worship that. Moses brings down instructions for the tabernacle where they will worship; when he sees their idolatrous behaviour, he smashes the stone tablets in anger and then pleads with God to save the people of Israel.

The instructions for the building of the tabernacle (Exodus 26—40) provide a way to get the Genesis 1 creation rhythms into their lives. Bezalel and Oholiab are the master builders chosen by God to oversee the work and teach others the skills required to build the tabernacle. Bezalel is filled with the creation spirit (*ruah Elohim*), the same spirit that moved over the face of the waters in Genesis 1. In Exodus 40:33, we are told that Moses 'finished the work'—the same phrase used of God's creation work in Genesis 2:2. Is this a coincidence? We are meant to see that Genesis 1 and 2 and Exodus 26—40 are the working out of creation and the way that we live.

The intimate connection between the world of creation and the world of worship is as significant today as it was when the tabernacle was first built in the wilderness. This connection between the world of creation and the world of worship is often ignored; for many it is obscured beyond recognition. The connection is totally lost when Christian people focus entirely on the end-times and the rapture. I would describe this as a creation-denying escape from time. It describes a condition that relentlessly pervades and secularizes a culture that has no context in creation.

The conditions in which God began to create are described in Genesis 1 as 'without form and void... darkness was upon the face of the deep' (v. 2, RSV). It was a black soup of nothingness, formless and empty: chaos. These continue to be the conditions in which creation takes place. The condition of the world today is like this. As I stand in the congregation, I feel that I am in the presence of something very much like this. I also believe that over the black abyss of watery chaos, the Spirit of God is moving, and breathing over the chaos of our current culture. There is a hint of a picture in the Genesis phrase of the Spirit of God 'moving' or 'hovering': the same verb is used in Deuteronomy 32:11 of an eagle nurturing or hovering over its young and its nest. The most well-known use of a bird to picture the moving Spirit of God is in the Gospel story of Jesus' baptism, in which we see the Spirit of God descending like a dove, followed by a voice from heaven saying, 'This is my beloved Son, with whom I am well pleased' (Matthew 3:17, NRSV).

These first Genesis words are lapidary, stark and spare. Creation takes place at the conjunction of a vast watery chaos and the Spirit of God. The Spirit of God is alive and present, descending upon and hovering over the chaos, and then the voice speaks: 'Let there be light', followed by seven more world-creating, life-creating verbs.

Every time I step into a pulpit in a church, or stand behind a lectern in a lecture hall, or sit in someone's kitchen talking about their lives, I am living out the conditions of Genesis 1, confronted by the formlessness and the void in people's lives in community and culture, but believing in the present and moving Spirit of God. Then the great life-creating gospel verbs are said and sung, verbs given their fullest articulation in Jesus. It's not just what pastors do; all of us do this—or can do it. Physicians say that they feel the same thing in their surgeries, farmers as they work their fields, parents as they look after their children. I can't imagine any work or condition in which the Genesis 1 text is not timely for reviving the sacred rhythms in which we are privileged to participate each and every day.

One of the most fulfilling things about being a pastor is entering the mess of a person's life—hearing, listening to and embracing it—praying, staying there day after day, year after year, and, in the process, hearing God whisper endless variations on 'Let there be...' and experiencing the coming together of one more detail of the creation and aspect of salvation, '... and it was so'. If we are going to be involved in God's creation work, we cannot avoid the mess. It cannot be denied, detoured, hurried through or procrastinated about. The mess—'without form and void'—is the biblical stuff of creation.

We must be present and enter the gift of rhythmic time in the midst of this mess, where the Spirit of God is moving and speaking creation and salvation into existence. When you write a poem, how many drafts do you throw away? When you paint a picture, how many tries before you get it right? When you get married, how many years does it take before you develop the habits of the heart and emotional maturity adequate for love? If you have a child, how long does it take you to get used to the absolute otherness of this life? Every creative act begins in the mess. Creation cannot be imposed mechanically on the mess.

Creation brings life, love and maturity out of darkness. It is how creation began and how creation continues and goes on around us as God's Spirit moves over the mess. It is both in us and all around us as God speaks heaven and earth into being. Everything we see and don't see is breathed into existence by God's word. There is so much around us to see, touch and taste; so much being desecrated, polluted and exploited by harassed and hurried men and women. 11 September 2001 is a great reminder of the chaos.

When we are trained in holy adoration, practised in the rhythms of a holy creation, the Sabbath-shaped week prepares us to give witness in detail of what happens when God speaks, and then to invite others to participate in receiving and caring for the whole of creation right now.

❖

PACIFIC SALMON: LINKING COASTAL FORESTS AND DEEP OCEANS

Leah Kostamo, A Rocha Canada

Few animals on Canada's Pacific Coast symbolize the link between forest and ocean eco-systems better than Pacific salmon. It's the old 'hip-bone-is-connected-to-the-thigh-bone' song and dance, but with an ecological twist, all done against the backdrop of one of creation's greatest migration cycles.

Beginning their lives in freshwater lakes, rivers and streams, the juvenile salmon spend a few months to a few years in fresh water before they head out to sea, where they will grow up to 23kg (50 pounds). The fare that enables them to pack on 98 per cent of their adult weight includes plankton, shrimp, anchovies and herring, to name a few.

At some point in each salmon's life, an instinctual bell goes off, telling it to return home. For some species this is relatively simple, as they have not ventured further than 150 miles from their home stream, but for others, like the Chinook who often travel as far as 2500 miles from their natal stream, it is an astounding feat. Not only do the vast majority of salmon migrate back to the stream in which they were spawned, but most make it within a few hundred metres of their birthplace. Scientists are unclear about how salmon find their way back to their natal stream, but evidently they use their sense of smell (a fish with a plugged nose can't find its way back).

Once back in fresh water, the drama heightens. Females return with bodies bulging with eggs. Males are often battered, with humped backs and torn fins, as they make the strenuous race against time to the spawning beds. The last leg of a salmon's life might seem macabre to those wanting to anthropomorphize their homecoming, but the spawning and subsequent death of salmon is one of the great connecting agents between the ecology of the ocean and that of the costal forests of western Canada. Some 22 species of mammals and birds feed directly on living or dead salmon, from grizzlies to bald eagles to stoneflies. And so the cycle goes, as nutrients from a saltwater shrimp are transferred to a migrating Chinook salmon, who loses the spawning race to a hungry grizzly, who leaves his droppings at the base of a Douglas fir seedling, which grows to a towering height thanks to the annual influx of fertilizer that coincides with the salmon run—and everyone scratches his or her head and wonders how that tree got so big, never dreaming it had anything to do with a measly shrimp.

Hazards abound for the Pacific salmon, threatening their habitat. Foremost among them are urbanization and resource extraction, which both lead to the loss of habitat in coastal British Columbia. A Rocha Canada has been working to protect and restore salmon habitat, in order to ensure that this amazing creature continues to thrive. In North Vancouver, we have been monitoring Coho salmon through spawner and fry surveys. In the Little Campbell River, just a few metres from A Rocha Canada's field study centre, we are working to restore habitat as well. A recent project removed a collapsed culvert from a tributary, opening up significant over-wintering habitat for Coho salmon. At the study centre itself, we are in the midst of a wetland restoration project, which we hope will provide food sources and possibly habitat for young salmon. In doing so, A Rocha is caring not only for one species in God's creation, but also for all the species that benefit from its survival.

GOD AND THE IMAGE BEARERS

John Houghton

It is often supposed that science and religion do not mix, that they are fundamentally in disagreement or even in conflict. There are two passages in the Judeo-Christian scriptures that I would like to consider to demonstrate that, on the contrary, true science and true religion go hand in hand and illuminate each other. Our first passage comes from the first chapter of the Bible in the book of Genesis and the second from one of David's compositions in the book of Psalms.

Then God said, 'Let us make man in our image, in our likeness, and let them rule over the fish of the sea and the birds of the air, over the livestock, over all the earth, and over all the creatures that move along the ground.' So God created man in his own image, in the image of God he created him; male and female he created them. God blessed them and said to them, 'Be fruitful and increase in number; fill the earth and subdue it. Rule over the fish of the sea and the birds of the air and over every living creature that moves on the ground.'
GENESIS 1:26–28

There are two main ideas in these three verses: first, that humans are made in God's image;[1] and second, that humans in God's image are given rule over the rest of creation. We look at these ideas in turn.

HUMANS IN GOD'S IMAGE

What does it mean that we are made in God's image? Many ideas are suggested by the word 'image'. First, being 'in God's image' means that we are God's representative and authority on earth; and second, to undertake this role we are endowed with God's Spirit. Most importantly, being God's representative implies a close relationship with God and also a close relationship with the rest of creation.

Humans—God's representatives

An ambassador represents his country in and to another country. To be a good ambassador, one needs detailed knowledge and understanding of both countries—their customs, culture, beliefs, history, capabilities and national characteristics. To be God's representative requires knowledge and understanding both of God and of his creation. The pursuit of science provides part of that knowledge and understanding. Today science is generally defined as knowledge of the natural world, but the root meaning of 'science' is 'knowledge', and in earlier times science was defined more broadly to include all objective knowledge (in other words, knowledge of things outside ourselves) and included God and the spiritual. Theology was even described as the 'queen of the sciences'.

The early chapters of Genesis provide illustrations of humans acquiring knowledge of creation. In Genesis 2:19, Adam names the animals, so distinguishing them one from the other and identifying their different characteristics—a scientific task. Taxonomy, the science or practice of plant and animal classification, was the earliest natural science. We also find in Genesis 2 that humans had learnt about the trees, those that were good for food (v. 9), and about minerals and precious stones (v. 12).

God has created us with minds that can explore and understand. Over the centuries our knowledge of creation has grown enormously and includes the science of the extremely large (the whole cosmos and its evolution since the big bang), the extremely small (the nuclei of atoms and their constituent parts) and the fundamental components of living systems (for example, their genetic make-up) with their remarkable variety. Albert Einstein once said that the most incomprehensible thing about the universe is that it is comprehensible.

Humans—endowed with God's Spirit

Being in God's image implies a close relationship with God. To enable that relationship, God gave Adam not only physical life but also spiritual life.

To mediate the spiritual life, God gives his Holy Spirit. We learn in the New Testament that Jesus is the human being who is the perfect human embodiment of God's image (Colossians 1:15) and who possessed the Holy Spirit in full measure.

To be in God's image means being like God (Genesis 1:26). God is the great Creator: he has conceived the whole universe, brought it into being and devised how it is ordered and how it functions. One of the ways in which we are to be like God is to be creative too: part of the endowment of God's Spirit is the ability to create. A biblical example of this is found in Exodus 31:1–6, where we find Bezalel 'filled... with the Spirit of God, with skill, ability and knowledge in all kinds of crafts—to make artistic designs for work in gold, silver and bronze, to cut and set stones, to work in wood, and to engage in all kinds of craftsmanship' (vv. 3–5), in order to build the tabernacle in the wilderness where God was to be especially present. Scientific knowledge is to be applied in technology for the benefit of humankind and for the whole of creation.

Humans as God's representatives given rule over creation

There has been much written about the meaning of the word 'rule' (translated 'dominion' in the AV) in Genesis 1:26 and 28. Some have argued[2] that much of the degradation of creation we find today stems from an interpretation of 'rule' as exploitation that ignores the damage being caused and fails to consider whether resources are being properly shared within the global human community. In Genesis 2:15, Adam is given more precise instructions as to his role with respect to creation and how to look after the garden of Eden. He was to 'work it and take care of it', the word used for 'work' having the meaning of service. The suggestion that rulers should also serve can be found in the idea of the servant-king in the Old Testament (for example, Psalm 72; and the servant songs in Isaiah), and above all in the Lordship of Jesus (Luke 22:27; John 13:13–15), who, 'taking the very nature of a servant... humbled himself' (Philippians 2:7–8). This sort of rule is often described by the word 'stewardship', a word used by Jesus to describe our role on earth (Luke 12:42, RSV). As stewards responsible to our Lord, we must act humbly with an attitude of service to creation, recognizing that we also are part of creation.

Because of human pride, greed and ignorance, there is a great temptation to use our knowledge and technology arrogantly, selfishly and thoughtlessly. The degradations we see in creation (air and water pollution, excess deforestation, soil erosion, climate change due to fossil fuel burning and so on) speak loudly of human mismanagement. Our rule over creation and our use of knowledge and technology must therefore be geared to the service of creation and pursued thoughtfully, honestly and humbly for the benefit of the whole of creation and that of our fellow humans and their particular needs.

In the first three chapters of Genesis, we find God taking great interest in his creation and in the responsibility for it that he had given to Adam and Eve. In 3:8 we find God walking in the garden 'in the cool of the day', with a strong hint that these walks were a regular occurrence. We can speculate about the conversations that God held with Adam and Eve as he learnt about their progress in understanding and care for creation. People sometimes suggest to me that the environmental problems we face in the world are too difficult for humans to solve. The message for us here is that we do not have to care for creation and solve these problems on our own. God is there beside us to help us and to provide the wisdom that we need.

PSALM 19

The two books

In the early days of experimental science in the 16th and 17th centuries, scientists such as Isaac Newton, Robert Boyle, John Ray and many others saw their pursuit of scientific knowledge as being for the glory of God. The idea was widely promulgated that God's revelation comes in the form of two books: the book of God's works (science) and the book of God's word (the Bible). It is generally believed to be Francis Bacon (1561–1626) who wrote, 'Let no man... think or maintain that a man can search too far or be too well studied in the book of God's word or in the book of God's works... but rather let men endeavour an endless progress of proficience in both.' But in fact the idea was developing much earlier. In particular, we find it in this remarkable Psalm 19, which C.S. Lewis described as 'the greatest poem in the Psalter and one of the greatest lyrics in the world'.[3]

The great Victorian preacher C.H. Spurgeon introduces this psalm of David as follows:

In his earliest days the psalmist while keeping his father's flock had devoted himself to the study of God's two great books—nature and scripture; and he had so thoroughly entered into the spirit of the two only volumes in his library that he was able with a devout criticism to compare and contrast them magnifying the excellency of the Author as seen in both.[4]

The first six verses present the magnificence, beauty, regularity and precision of God's works in creation that is universally available—everyone can see it. The laws of nature are the Creator's laws and show his glory. The next three verses (vv. 6–9) contain brief but instructive *hexapla* (Greek, meaning 'sixfold') about God's word, containing six descriptive titles, six characteristic qualities and six divine effects.

Verses 10–11 enthuse about the value of the book of God's word, and the final three verses encourage us to apply the word to our personal actions (both hidden and wilful sins are addressed), words and thoughts.

David puts the two books of God's revelation alongside each other without apology or explanation. In doing so, he draws a clear parallel between God's 'laws' that control the physical universe with all their intricacy and precision, and God's moral laws that regulate human behaviour and relationships both within the human family and towards the divine Creator.

David had only a small fragment of the word in the books of Moses. We have so very much more: we have the whole Bible. In particular, we have the person of Jesus, the perfect image of God, the Son of man and Son of God, who became part of creation. He is described by John (John 1:1–3) both as the Word of God and also as the agent of the whole creation. God's two books come together in the unique revelation of God in Jesus.

We live in a world where God is ignored, the Bible is unknown, God's rules are not followed, and people do their own thing, think what they want and believe what they like. When the world is seen in this subjective way, facts are ignored and even the objective truth of science is questioned and viewed as just another opinion. Psalm 19 places the objectivity of both natural law and moral law alongside each other. We are encouraged to revel in the excellence of both; we are bound to obey the former, and the imperative of the latter demands our obedience too. The psalm ends as

David very beautifully prays for God's help with that obedience, so that he can be completely in tune with God's revelation as presented in both of his books.

WRESTLING WITH PEOPLE AND ELEPHANTS

Vijay D. Anand, A Rocha India

'Elephants Invade City' blazed the newspaper headlines on 29 January 1985. Students of a local college near Bangalore city woke up to find a herd of elephants outside their building. This incursion into human habitations is nothing new. It has been going on since people began to cultivate the land within the forested areas. By and large, people in India have tolerated the problems related to living alongside wildlife, but the recent struggle for space has proved more problematic.

As one of the world's 17 mega-diversity countries in ecological terms, India has an estimated forest cover of 19.39 per cent of the total geographical area. It is incredibly rich in biodiversity, which proves that the people and wildlife have, until recently, co-existed relatively peace-fully. Today, the story is different. The survival of many species is being threatened by a human population explosion that is putting tremendous pressure on the ecosystems and causing increasing competition for space. More than 580,000 villages in and around the forests of India, with a population of 140 million people, are dependent on forest products. The resulting heavy pressure on the ecosystems has led to multi-dimensional social and environmental problems.

Bannerghatta National Park is a classic example. Located 24km from Bangalore in India's Silicon Valley, the park is a narrow strip of forest (104 square kilometres) surrounded by nearly 120 villages. The park is contiguous to the forests of south India and is home to a variety of flora and fauna, including the majestic Asian elephant. In most of the countries that the Asian elephant inhabits, it is seen as a flagship for conservation. As the largest land mammal, it warrants conservation; and as the carrier of valuable ivory, it warrants legal protection too. Even though the highest level of protection by the Indian Wildlife Protection Act is in operation, the survival of the elephant continues to be threatened by various issues. Perhaps one of the most severe of these issues is the conflict between the elephant and the local human population, both of whom are struggling for survival.

A Rocha India has been working to study the human–elephant conflict issues at the park. In order to ensure the continued existence of the Asian elephant, it is important to reduce all of the threats to its survival. Many conservationists, however, ignore the need to link their conservation initiatives with potential improvements to the quality of life for the local people. Similarly, those working in rural development have often paid scant attention to the need to maintain functioning ecosystems that, in the end, are essential to improving human lifestyles.

An indication of the conflict between the local community and the wildlife is seen in an annual study. The study showed that, on average, nearly 10,000 US dollars worth of crops and livestock are lost and about four people killed each year. The government compensation scheme does not match the actual financial loss, and the loss of life can never be recompensed. Various methods of conflict mitigation have been unsuccessful for a number of reasons. The local indigenous people depend on the forest for their fuel and fodder needs, yet the protected status of the national parks and wildlife sanctuaries, particularly for the elephant, has made accessibility to forest resources difficult.

The enormous potential for the forests to contribute to the well-being of the rural community should be viewed in the context of the grinding poverty faced by these people. Unfortunately the conservation of wildlife has failed to bring a fuller appreciation of the value of biological diversity among the various stakeholders. Now the conflict between the conservation efforts and the necessity to meet the legitimate needs of the local people has exploded. A balance needs to be found between the strategies that guide the conservation of the natural habitat and the everyday requirements of the local indigenous people. While the force of the law protects the elephants and other wildlife, it is worth remembering that the forest will only be preserved through the participation of local communities. At the same time, it is the local communities that have a vested interest in the continued survival of the ecosystems for their own livelihood.

A Rocha believes that, through education, the local communities can learn to appreciate the sensitive ecological landscape that they inhabit and once again work within its limitations and its diversity to conserve the whole of the forest areas. It is not always easy working in a culturally, socially and religiously diverse and sensitive society like India. At A Rocha India, however, we believe that this is where we are called to work— between environmental conservation and meeting the legitimate needs and aspirations of poor human communities.

FURTHER READING

David Atkinson, *The Message of Genesis 1—11* (IVP, 1990).
R.J. Berry (ed.), *The Care of Creation* (IVP, 2000).
R.J. Berry, *God's Book of Works* (T&T Clark, 2003).
Henri Blocher, *In the Beginning* (IVP, 1984).
David Wilkinson, *The Message of Creation* (IVP, 2002).

REJECTION OF THE CREATOR

R.J. (Sam) Berry

Four centuries ago, Galileo challenged the traditional scriptural under-standing that the Earth was the central fixed point of the universe, surrounded by orbiting planets. He wrote (1616), 'The Bible teaches us how to go to heaven, not how the heavens go.' It is said that 'it was Galileo's telescope, not his church, that conclusively refuted the inter-pretation of Psalm 96:10 "The earth is firmly established, it cannot be moved" as a proof-text against the earth's rotation'.

Given the challenge that science presents to traditional biblical inter-pretation of scripture, what are we to make of the story in Genesis 3 about the disobedience of Adam and Eve in a paradisaical Eden and the resulting curse upon the earth? Are there any alternatives to interpreting it either as literal history or rejecting it as mere myth, inconsistent with the facts of human development known to science, especially with evolution?

ADAM: MAN OR MYTH?

The Bible seems to intend us to accept Adam and Eve as historical figures. The biblical genealogies trace the human race back to Adam (Genesis 5:3; 1 Chronicles 1:1; Luke 3:38), Jesus taught the basis of marriage as that 'at the beginning the Creator "made them male and female"' (Matthew 19:4), and Paul told the Athenian philosophers that God had made every nation 'from one man' (Acts 17:26). Particularly important in the present context, Paul's carefully constructed analogy between Adam and Christ depends on the equal historicity of both (Romans 5:12–19; see also 1 Corinthians 15:21, 45); it is unconvincing to suggest that Paul was talking in these passages about 'corporate humanity' or treating Adam as a universal 'mythical man'.

Adam's disobedience and God's curse

The first rule of Bible interpretation is to interpret scripture with scripture. The problem is that the events of Genesis 3 are not directly referred to elsewhere in the older Testament. Traditionally, in Judaism, there is no strong doctrine of the fall. Clearly we are sinners in need of reconciliation with our God, but the emphasis in Judaism is on individual responsibility for personal failings; neither the rabbinic nor the Jewish apocalyptic tradition recognizes the idea of a cosmic fall involving the whole of creation.

Both Testaments refer often to divine control over the natural world, such as over wind and sea (Exodus 10:13–19; Numbers 11:31; Job 26:12; Psalm 107:25, 29; 135:7; Isaiah 50:2; Jeremiah 5:22; 49:32–36; Amos 4:13; Nahum 1:4; Mark 4:37–39), although this is not given as an answer to the disorder prescribed by the curses of Genesis 3. The clearest commentary on Genesis 3 is Romans 8:19–22, where Paul speaks of the creation being 'subjected to frustration, not by its own choice, but by the will of the one who subjected it' (that is to say, God), and of 'the whole creation... groaning' while waiting for our adoption as sons.

This is not an event in the distant future. The whole middle section of Romans is concerned with justification and restoration through Christ. The creation 'groaning' as a result of Adam's disobedience is dealt with through the 'revealing' of the sons of God (Romans 8:19). But only a few verses earlier, Paul had stated that 'those who are led by the Spirit of God *are* sons of God... The Spirit himself testifies with our spirit that we *are* God's children' (vv. 14, 16). In other words, the groaning of creation finds its answer in the justifying work of Christ, a connection made directly in the Colossian letter, where we are told that 'God was pleased... through [Christ] to reconcile to himself *all things*, whether things on earth or things in heaven, by making peace through his blood, shed on the cross' (Colossians 1:19–20).

The rejection of the Creator that took place in Eden was dealt with by Christ's atoning death at Calvary; the fall is a prelude to the gospel. It is an explicitly and gloriously Christian doctrine, but can we reconcile it with science?

SCIENCE AND THE FALL

It is all very well to argue that the fall finds its remedy in Christ's atoning death. That is implicit in the Genesis passage itself, where the serpent is told that the offspring of the woman will crush its head (Genesis 3:15), but how should we understand the story against the background of the 21st century? Do we have to allegorize it completely? Can we justify it as, in some sense, a historical account?

The fall is an interconnected story in seven 'scenes' (2:5–17; 2:18–25; 3:1–5; 3:6–8; 3:9–13; 3:14–21; 3:22–24), arranged in the common Hebraic pattern of chiasmus: scene 1 is paired with scene 7, 2 with 6, and so on. The centrepiece is scene 4, when the couple eat the forbidden fruit. It has been described as 'proto-history'. What actually happened? It is helpful to recognize three stages.

1. Adam: a two-stage creation

Adam was a neolithic farmer, living close to the start of the Bronze Age (Genesis 4:22) as urbanization was beginning (4:17). Genesis 2 makes it clear that he led a settled existence in the Near East; one son was an agriculturist, a second was a shepherd (4:2). All this dates him around 10,000–15,000 years ago. How does this fit with the millions of years of human fossil ancestry, or the fact that by the time farming and non-nomadic existence were beginning in the Near East, there were already humans (*Homo sapiens*) in the Americas and Asia?

The answer is found not in science, but in the Bible's description of Adam himself: alone among the animals, Adam is said to be in God's 'image' and 'likeness' (Genesis 1:26, 27). Whatever this means, it certainly has nothing to do with anatomy or genetics. The obvious solution (and one which is entirely consistent with scripture) is that God put ('breathed') his own 'image' into the body of an existing animal; indeed, Genesis 2:7 implies that Adam was a 'two-stage' creation, with something previously created being transformed through spiritual 'in-breathing'.

This means that it is proper to distinguish pre-Adamic humans, which constitute the species known to biologists and anthropologists as *Homo sapiens*, from Adam and his successors, whom we can call *Homo divinus*. Furthermore, the creation of *Homo divinus* was a divine act, and thus not subject to the familiar time and space constraints of Mendelian genetics and sexual reproduction: we can envisage God's unique act of the creation of *Homo divinus* in Adam as spreading to all *Homo sapiens* alive at the time. This is, and will be, speculative, but it accords fully with the biblical record and does not conflict in any way with scientific understanding.

2. The death of Adam and Eve

Adam and Eve, the original members of *Homo divinus*, were forbidden to eat from the tree(s?) of good and evil and life 'in the middle of the garden' (Genesis 2:9, 17; 3:3). Disobedience would mean death (2:17; 3:3). But Adam and Eve did eat the forbidden fruit. The result was alienation from God (3:7–10) and banishment from his presence (3:23). Adam and Eve died in the sense of being separated from God, the source of life. They did not die in the biological sense because they lived on for many years and had all their children after their exclusion from Eden (4:1—5:5).

This distinction between physical and spiritual death is necessary if we are to make sense of Christ's redeeming work. Paul tells the Ephesians, '*you were dead* in your transgressions and sins' but God 'made us alive with Christ' (Ephesians 2:1, 5); and he wrote to the Colossians in almost the same words: '*When you were dead* in your sins… God made you alive with Christ' (Colossians 2:13). It is implicit in Christ's admonition to Nicodemus about the need to be 'born again' (John 3:3–7). What is the relationship between physical and spiritual death? Would Adam and Eve have survived for ever if they had not disobeyed God? These are real questions, but they should not lead us to assume that physical and spiritual death are identical. 'For if, by the trespass of the one man, death reigned through that one man, how much more will those who receive God's abundant provision of grace and of the gift of righteousness reign in life through the one man, Jesus Christ' (Romans 5:17).

3. Evidence for the curse

How does the non-human creation fit into this picture? If the fundamental effect of the fall was human separation from God, what is the 'curse' that

God put on the ground (Genesis 3:17–18)? (Note that neither the man nor the woman was cursed. Their sentences were disruption in their appointed roles: for the woman, the relationship of 'love and cherish' became 'desire and dominate'; for the man, the land is cursed 'until you return to the ground', v. 19—usually taken to mean physical death, but it could imply the need to take up again the task of stewardship laid upon Adam.) There is no evidence of any ecological or environmental change in neolithic times, nor that 'thorns and thistles' (or, for that matter, carnivory) appeared around the same time. The appearance of thorns and thistles gives us a clue to the curse: thorns and thistles are weeds, and weeds are not intrinsically evil; they are merely plants growing in the wrong place. They indicate uncared-for land.

This brings us back to the 'groaning' and 'frustrated' creation. Charles Cranfield has dealt with these descriptions in a powerful *reductio ad absurdum* argument:

What sense can there be in saying that 'the sub-human creation—the Jungfrau, for example, or the Matterhorn, or the planet Venus—suffers frustration by being prevented from properly fulfilling the purpose of its existence'? The answer must surely be that the whole magnificent theatre of the universe, together with all its splendid properties and all its life, created for God's glory, is cheated of its full fulfilment so long as man, the chief actor in the great drama of God's praise, fails to contribute his rational part. The Jungfrau and the Matterhorn and the planet Venus and all living things too, man alone excepted, do indeed glorify God in their own ways; but, since their praise is destined to be not a collection of individual offerings but part of a magnificent whole, the united praise of the whole creation, they are prevented from being fully that which they were created to be, so long as man's part is missing, just as all the other players in a concerto would be frustrated of their purpose if the soloist were to fail to play his part.[1]

Derek Kidner uses the same analogy in his commentary on Genesis:

Leaderless, the choir of creation can only grind on in discord. It seems from Romans 8:19–23 and from what is known of the pre-human world that there was a state of travail in nature from the first, which man was empowered to 'subdue' until he relapsed into disorder himself.[2]

God described his creation as 'finished' from his point of view (Genesis 2:2), but he had already given our first parents dominion and the responsibility of tilling and taking care of the ground (Genesis 1:28; 2:15); our world was (and is) certainly 'very good', but not 'perfect' in the sense of a museum exhibit. By disobeying God's very first command, we have failed to prevent ecological disorder; indeed, we have effectively colluded with the devil in worsening it. Henri Blocher summarizes it well: 'If man obeys God, he would be the means of blessing the earth; but in his insatiable greed… and in his short sighted selfishness, he pollutes and destroys it. He turns the garden into a desert (cf. Rev. 11:18). That is the main thrust of the curse of Genesis 3.'[3]

GOD'S JUDGMENT: OUR PART

God made us to glorify him and to care for his creation on his behalf. Sadly, the first recorded decision of *Homo divinus* was to disobey God and fail in their stewardship. We have not only made a mess of our world but, disastrously, we behave as if it did not matter; we have ignored God and treated him as unnecessary and irrelevant. We are justly condemned, and alienated from God. The relationship for which we were created can only be restored by God himself. Marvellously, 'God so loved the world [the Greek word translated 'world' is *cosmos*] that he gave his one and only Son, that whoever believes in him shall not perish but have eternal life' (John 3:16); Christ's death at Calvary reconciled 'all things' to the Father (Colossians 1:20). Christ's atoning death not only made possible the restoration of our relationship with the Father (John 1:12), it also makes us whole by removing the alienation that we experience with ourselves, our neighbours, and with the rest of creation.

Lynn White was Professor of History at the University of California in 1966 when, in a lecture to the American Association for the Advancement of Science, he notoriously described the Christian attitude to creation as being 'superior to nature, contemptuous of it, willing to use it for our slightest whim'. He was writing about fallen man (and woman). Intriguingly, he went on, 'Since the roots of our present trouble are so largely religious, the remedy must also be essentially religious, whether we call it that or not'—which is where biblical faith leads us. Redeemed man (and woman) can join in a hymn with all creation: 'You are worthy, our Lord and God, to receive glory and honour and power, for you created all things, and by your will they were created and have their being' (Revelation 4:11).

THE ISLES OF SCILLY:
HEARING GOD'S CALL

Dave Bookless, A Rocha UK

What does it take to change the direction of somebody's life? Most thinking people, including many Christians, have some concern about the state of the planet, but what does it take to change that generalized, slightly guilty concern into decisive, life-changing action?

In 1989 I was training for ordained Christian ministry in the Anglican Church. If you had told my wife and me then that we would end up leaving full-time church leadership for the uncertainty of setting up the UK branch of a Christian environmental charity, we would have been amused certainly, intrigued perhaps, but mostly incredulous. Yet, in God's unexpected leading, that's where we are.

The first turning point that made this possible took place during a family holiday on the Isles of Scilly. The Scillies are a group of small low-lying islands around a shallow lagoon, 28 miles off Land's End. Warmed by the Gulf Stream, the climate is mild and the islands are famous for spring flowers, sandy beaches, abundant marine wildlife and rare migrant birds. We were self-catering on St Martin's, a small island with a resident population of about 60. After a wonderful fortnight, swimming in the warm sea, lying on the beach reading, eating fresh fish, watching seals, puffins and migrating waders, we had created a fair amount of rubbish, so we asked how to dispose of it. We were told to burn paper and card, but to take any packaging, tins, bottles and plastics to 'the tip' at one end of the island.

With our bags full of waste, we walked across springy rabbit-mown turf dotted with pink flowers, past wheeling gulls and near-empty beaches, until we reached the path's end. In front of us was a small cliff and a rocky bay containing 'the tip'—rusting cars and tractors, mouldy cans, fragments of glass and multi-coloured bits of plastic blowing about, with a few large rats ambling lazily around. The contrast with our idyllic surroundings came over us like a cloud obscuring the sun, and we silently added our wastefulness to the piles below. As we did so, I sensed God speaking—not audibly, but so clearly that the words became imprinted in my mind: 'How do you think I feel about what you're doing to my world?'

'How do you think I feel about what you're doing to my world?' The question provoked Anne and me to do three things. First, we went back to the Bible, where we were shocked by the clarity of God's ownership and involvement in creation, and of our responsibility as caretakers. Second, we examined our lifestyles, where our own wastefulness—hidden by weekly refuse collections and well-concealed landfill sites—caused us to take small steps towards living more simply. Finally, we sought out other Christians who were already on this journey of biblical discovery and soon came across A Rocha. We visited the A Rocha centre, Cruzinha in Portugal, and found a group of people open to God, each other and the creation, committed both to enjoying God in studying his handiwork and also to obeying God in protecting his world. The rest, as they say, is history.

FURTHER READING

H. Blocher, *In the Beginning* (IVP, 1984).

H. Blocher, *Original Sin* (Apollos, 1997).

W.S. Brown, N. Murphy and H.N. Malony (eds), *Whatever Happened to the Soul?* (Fortress, 1998).

E. Brunner, *Man in Revolt* (Lutterworth, 1939).

D. Kidner, *Genesis*, Tyndale Old Testament Commentaries (IVP, 1967).

G.J. Wenham, *Genesis 1—15*, World Bible Commentary (Word, 1987).

GOD'S COVENANT WITH THE EARTH

Peter Harris

God's covenant with Noah was a commitment to maintain the inherent relationship between Creator and creation; his relationship with the natural order—implicit in the act of creation—whereby he promised never again to destroy the earth with a flood. This divine pledge, given unconditionally to Noah and to every living creature on earth, was accompanied by the sign of the rainbow.

The story of God's covenant with Noah has more relevance in our times than it has ever had before. In a world torn apart by injustice, oppression, wars and environmental degradation, we are perhaps the first generation to read it with such a sober understanding of the destruction with which it begins (Genesis 6:5), and such a sharp awareness of the vital importance of the promise of God with which it ends (9:8–17). The same can be said for some of the forebodings of the Old Testament prophets who understood that living selfishly and independently from God brought about not only human but also ecological catastrophe, which was the direct consequence of human disobedience of God.[1]

We often read these Genesis passages from a merely human perspective, yet their relevance is more far-reaching. We read them at a time when, according to the best studies, up to a quarter of the species of animals and plants of which we are aware, and with which we share this earth, face extinction in the next 50 years.[2] The rates vary, but all are many times higher than the natural rate of extinction, and all are directly related to human activity and choices.

In this terrible present predicament, the ark becomes a potent symbol of the human role in God's rescue effort, and the rainbow shines as a precious promise of hope for the creation itself. If we are looking for answers to the current state of the planet, and in particular its catastrophic loss of biodiversity, we must understand the story of the flood as more than a story about the human condition, although the person and family of Noah stand at its heart. In Genesis 9, where God promises a future and a hope, the promise is for the whole creation. Furthermore, as commentator Bruce Waltke has pointed out, 'The intentional repetition of the phrases "every living creature" and "all life" eight times in verses 8–17 alone affirms God's desire to preserve every species. The human annihilation of species is a matter of grave concern to the Creator.'[3]

While the place of people in the future promise of God's care and protection is central, it is intentionally extended to the rest of life on earth. This focus stands in direct contrast to the Near Eastern pagan and polytheistic creation stories of the ancient world at the time Genesis was written; Genesis records it as a covenant between God and all life on earth (9:17).

Biblical covenant language, and the force of stories such as the flood, should call our attention to the way that we have allowed ourselves to interpret biblical texts and to take on a view of life that is not entirely in keeping with orthodox biblical Christian belief. In Western thinking, over the last 500 years at least, a reordering has taken place based on the idea of a distant, or finally illusory, Creator God, and an increasingly potent human presence taking centre stage in the drama of history. In societies that have accepted this view, it has become difficult for the Christian church not to read and interpret biblical history as simply human history, and ignore God's commitment to all that he has made. In order to redress this shift in thinking and to do justice to the biblical account of the flood, we need to reconsider the way we see things and align ourselves to the biblical understanding of humanity as created by God.

In outline, the flood story shows us God distressed and finally outraged by human wickedness. He resolves to make a new start with the only family to obey and trust him, and to give into its care representatives of current biodiversity on earth. Following the destruction and symbolic baptism of the earth that the flood brings, God commits himself never again to take such drastic measures, and to persist in protecting and providing for Noah, his family and all life on earth.

As we have read and believed in God's promises, the story that has, of course, most interested us is about our human well-being, but the irony is that in most times and places we have gone on to secure it at the cost of the rest of life on earth. Whereas Noah's faith and technology were put at the service of all creation, which was then physically taken into his survival story, our own faith and technology follow the humanism of recent centuries in taking little account of the well-being of the wider creation. Even more scandalously in view of the fact that, as Genesis would see it, we are literally 'all in the same boat', our human comfort has been secured by driving the poor into further poverty, to the point where more than half the world currently lives on less than a dollar a day, where over a billion people have no access to water of drinkable quality, and where the demands we make individually on the resources of creation can vary by up to 40 times depending on where and how we live.

This human suffering cries out to the Creator as it did in the time of Noah. The Church worldwide is, for the most part, not indifferent to the need to work for change, but is not entirely convinced of its place in the priorities of mission. But we have to acknowledge that, despite the essential place in God's concerns that Genesis and other books in both Testaments give to the well-being of the wider creation, we have remained stubbornly interested only in the human part of the story. If God insists on his covenant with creation, what might it mean for us to live out our own covenant? To find out, we must look again at what the covenant implied.

RECOVERING AN UNDERSTANDING OF THE COVENANT

The first vital component of a covenant, and its starting point, is the idea that it must be based on an agreement with a worthy partner. We find this idea both before the fall, in the ringing affirmations of the first chapters of Genesis that the creation is good, and afterwards, in the idea that creation's redemption was worth the life of God's own Son. God was pleased with what he made, and Jesus died to reconcile all things to himself (Colossians 1:20).

In contrast to this, Christian history has a chequered record with the idea of the goodness and worth of creation, and, through the centuries, has ranged over all the possibilities. Leaving aside questions of biodiversity for a moment, we can understand how the Church has engaged with the question of the physical and material world by looking at another area altogether. These varying attitudes can be seen most sharply in the Christian treatment of the question of sex in different communities through the centuries. William May's four categories of sex, seen at different times by the Church as demonic, divine, casual or as simply a nuisance, might well stand as a convenient shorthand for some deformations of the Church's general understanding of creation itself.[4]

However we understand the physical world, we need to recognize that often we have not been able to give creation the free-standing place that the Noah covenant in Genesis describes. Too frequently we have attempted to establish a value for creation and life on earth only in so far as it meets our own needs, and so placed ourselves too prominently in the agreement between God and life on earth. But God made his agreement because what he created was good and was brought into being in love, first for his glory and then for our good. Only in that framework was it entrusted to human care.

The second vital component in the covenant is harder to understand and reflects the conditions that must remain on both sides for the covenant to be valid. Here again, though, people are firmly put in their place, and this stands as a necessary counter to our current sense of our central place in the scheme of things. Although human folly and wickedness led to the ecological devastation of God's judgment in the flood and, later, through the fulfilment of the prophets' words,[5] God does not tie the destiny of all life on earth to human folly. Rather, he assures creation that his care will continue regardless of human sin. So the covenant gives us a very practical form of hope, even now in the face of some of the more disastrous consequences of our abuse of the earth and its species.

As we look at the covenant as an expression of God's relationship to the earth, we are given an intensely practical way of living faithfully and in a proper relationship to the wider world. The true value of other life on earth is that it is created and cared for by a personal Creator. It is not merely raw material for economic growth, or semi-divine emanations of some impersonal creative force, or, even worse, our enemy in the struggle for species dominance, to be subdued in our fight to survive.

It is precisely the confusion over what status to give to the rest of creation that has led to the incoherence of our relationships with our environment. We can also find in the covenant our proper place as earth-keepers for the living God who holds all creation together. The covenant is given expression by Noah and his family; and the Church, which is the body of Christ the Creator, stands in their line to live out God's care and love for all he has made.

In Exodus, God shows his continuing love and concern for his people as he promises to lead them out of slavery in Egypt into the land that he has prepared for them to inhabit. The theme of the Sinai covenant between God and his people helps us to understand God's promise of salvation and redemption. The covenant required obedience to the Ten Commandments, and the Old Testament in general. The land of Canaan, promised to Abraham in Genesis 17:8, is an integral part of the Sinai covenant as Moses leads the people of Israel through the wilderness to the land of Canaan, which was to be their inheritance. Disobedience to God and his law, and breaking the covenant, would lead to exile from the land (Deuteronomy 28:36), disease, drought and crop failure (Leviticus 26:15–20). Here we see that creation is drawn into the rebellions of God's people. We also see the promised redemption brought about through the people's repentance as they hear the message of God's forgiveness and renewed love in the words of Ezekiel and Isaiah (Isaiah 61—65 and Ezekiel 47—48). Despite the rebellious nature of God's people, God never abandoned his love for all he had made, even when it was spoilt and scarred by human disobedience.

Today we live under a new covenant, which is the fulfilment of God's purposes of salvation, expressed in the Old Testament covenants. It is a covenant of grace mediated by Jesus Christ through his sacrificial death and resurrection. The new covenant promises the redemption of the whole of creation, forgiveness and a renewed relationship with God through the Holy Spirit.

We need to rediscover, in the practice of living in the times and places God gives us, what the hope of this new covenant means. By thinking in terms of the covenant, we see what folly it is to attempt to graft on environmental issues as just one issue for the Church's social agenda. Rather, the task that faces us is to restore the biblical place of all life on earth in our thinking, and to translate God's concerns into our own discipleship as we follow Jesus the Lord, the Creator, whom New Testament scholar Rikk Watts has called 'the first earth-keeper'.[6] In the terms of secular society, the Church is the biggest non-government organization in the world,[7] and so we can glimpse what could be some wonderful consequences for all life on earth if we return to our true calling to be the body of Christ, and a biblical grasp of the scope of the gospel.

SAVING ENDEMIC SPECIES

Chris Magero, A Rocha Kenya

The sunrise in Watamu, Kenya, spreads glistening rays across the Indian Ocean. Dazzling and beautiful, they glimmer on the water's surface. A few kilometres down the coastline is Mida Creek, a gorgeous inlet leading into Mida village. Immediately inland from Mida stands the Arabuko-Sokoke forest, the largest remaining fragment of coastal forest in eastern Africa. Only 420 square kilometres of it now remains.

As you walk along the animal tracks under the canopies of the *Brachystegia* and *Cynometra* forest, you may hear the call of the Amani sunbird break the serene silence. Her call merges with other bird calls, including the sizzling cries of a flock of Clarke's weavers. You might also be lucky enough to see the golden rumped elephant-shrew scrambling through the undergrowth, or the Sokoke pipit. These species, found almost nowhere else in the world, are either entirely endemic to Arabuko-Sokoke forest or very nearly so. They find their refuge in this forest.

Mida Creek is similarly important, being home to five of Africa's six mangrove species. It is also 'temporary home' to wading birds, flocking in their thousands during the northern winter, including the crab-plover, which has been adopted as A Rocha Kenya's logo. Loss of this habitat would lead to the decline of certain populations of these species because, with changing land use increasingly limiting their feeding and roosting grounds, they will have nowhere else to go in the winter.

Despite the beauty and richness of the forest and creek, they face tremendous pressure from illegal exploitation. Most people are unaware of the fact that the forest holds such precious, yet threatened, plants and animals, and equally unaware of the importance of Mida Creek for migrant birds. Persistent logging is leading to the loss of indigenous trees, among them the precious *muhuhu* tree, the hollows of which are used by the elephant-shrew as a home. These areas have been designated as a UNESCO Biosphere Reserve and as Important Bird Areas (IBAs), but practical solutions still have to be sought to ensure their survival.

Through initiating a project called ASSETS (Arabuko Sokoke Schools and Eco-Tourism Scheme), A Rocha Kenya have stepped in, offering a solution. Local people who exploit the forest do so largely due to poverty and in order to pay for basic needs, such as education. ASSETS offers scholarships to children living within 4km of the forest edge, who have qualified for secondary education. An educated people are an empowered people, and thus will in future carry on looking after their environment.

The funds for these scholarships come from eco-tourism and from donations, and therefore depend on tourists coming to visit. Families of the supported children are told how the scheme works, and are encouraged to refrain from cutting down trees, trapping wild animals for meat and sale, or exploiting Mida Creek by using under-sized mesh fishing nets. They are also encouraged to plant trees as an alternative source of energy or income. In so doing, the flow of tourists will be maintained in the area but the species will be conserved as well.

Working alongside ASSETS is A Rocha Kenya's Environmental Education Programme, operating both in schools and the wider community. The programme works among young and old, educating them about the importance of the forest and the creek. Science teachers are also taught how to include examples about taking care of the environment within their normal national curriculum syllabus.

With 94 children and their families benefiting from ASSETS eco-bursaries, people's attitudes towards the forest and creek are changing. Many now see the forest as a source of something good and not just a source of crop-destroying elephants and baboons. There is much still to do, but the future for the Arabuko-Sokoke forest and Mida Creek is looking much brighter.

SABBATH FOR THE LAND AND JUBILEE

Chris Wright

We enjoy time, we are carried along in the flow of time, everything is embedded in its time, so the very idea of exploiting the flow of time to take interest on money lent seems preposterous. It does so no more because the sacredness of time has disappeared, even before the sacredness of the land vanished from the memories of our modern societies. Instead capitalist market economies have been elevated to global importance; they are enshrined with the qualities of omnipotence that border on idolatory. So the question arises: does it make sense to attribute to money qualities that no created thing can ever have, namely eternal growth? Every tree must die, every house must one day crumble, every human being must perish. Why should immaterial goods such as capital—and its counterpart, debts—not also have their time? The capital knows no natural barriers to its growth. There is no jubilee to put an end to its accumulative power. And so there is no jubilee to put an end to debts and slavery. Money that feeds on money, with no productive or social obligation, represents a vast flood that threatens even large national economies and drowns small countries… But at the heart of this deregulation is the undisputed concept of the eternal life of money.
GEIKO MULLER-FAHRENHOLZ[1]

Debt is one of the main causes of social disintegration, breeding poverty, squalor, crime and violence. Debt is not a modern phenomenon, however, and it is understood most profoundly in the history of Israel revealed through the Old Testament. In my view, Lutheran minister and writer Geiko Muller-Fahrenholz presents an interesting and convincing view of the principles behind the Old Testament institution of jubilee. He contrasts the commercializing of time in modern debt—and interest-based economies—with the potent theology of time implied in the sabbatical cycles of Israel. It was for very good reason that the worldwide campaign to end the debt of impoverished nations was called Jubilee 2000.

The year of jubilee is an Old Testament institution deeply rooted in Israel's theology of the land, which plays a major role in the overall faith of Israel. In order to understand the principles and theology of jubilee and its relevance to Christian ethics and mission, it is helpful to look at three complementary and mutually reinforcing perspectives: the social, economic and theological angles. Then we shall explore Leviticus 25 in order to understand the legislation itself. Finally we shall look at the potential for a jubilee within Christian ethics using three different ways, two of which—the paradigmatic and eschatological methods of interpretation—come from within the Old Testament itself. The third, the typological, is taken from a New Testament perspective.[2]

The *paradigmatic* approach assumes that God's relationship with Israel in their land was intended to be a reflection in microcosm of God's relationship to humanity on earth. This means that we must take seriously the objectives of the Old Testament texts that explain the social and economic laws of Israel if we are to use these texts as models to understand the laws in a 21st-century society.

The *eschatological* approach assumes that God's redemptive design for Israel and the land is a prototype that will ultimately extend to all nations, when the whole earth will be transformed into the new creation. The Old Testament looks forward to the whole of humanity accepting God's rule and also the whole created order of the world being transformed. God will not abandon his creation. He will redeem it (see Deuteronomy 11:12; 28:1–14; Leviticus 26:12). The function of the land with Israel points to the 'new heaven and new earth' in which God will dwell with his people. This parallels the 'new Jerusalem' in the New Testament (compare Revelation 21:1–5). How, then, should we live in the midst of this redemptive story?

The *typological* approach recognizes that Jesus as the Messiah fulfilled the mission of Israel and is the embodiment of the people of God. This means that the believer in Christ is the spiritual seed of Abraham and therefore heir to God's promises, and that the Christian Church stands in spiritually organic continuity with Old Testament Israel (Galatians 3:26–28). If the land is so important in Old Testament theology, where does it fit into the New Testament? Certainly the relevance of the land as a holy place is not seen in the New Testament; nor is the vocabulary of the land being a gift or a blessing or a promised inheritance. In part, this is because of the rapid spread of the Church across nations and borders. More importantly, Christ took into himself the holiness of the land and all the attributes of promise and gift in the Old Testament. Christ's spiritual presence sanctifies any place where believers are present. The promise of Jesus to be present wherever his people meet (Matthew 18:20; 28:20) embraces and completes the Old Testament promise of God's presence among his people (Genesis 28:15).

The function of the land in the life and faith of Israel was a symbolic proof to the Israelite householder of the covenant relationship with God. The land was God's gift and a fulfilment of his promise to Abraham. Deuteronomy speaks of the land as Israel's inheritance. It was evidence of their relationship with God, and the land itself was the place of life with God. It meant security, blessing, sharing and responsibility. In this three-fold framework for interpretation, paradigmatic, typological and eschato-logical approaches are not independent of one another but interrelated. If we affirm a typological relationship between the land of Israel and the community of Christian believers, then our paradigmatic appreciation of Israel's relationship to the land will form and strengthen our appreciation for the social and economic responsibilities of Christian fellowship. Similarly, our eschatological understanding informs our confidence and hope in God's ultimate victory over fallen creation. That understanding and belief becomes the rationale for our application of biblical principles to economic and ecological issues in the world today.

If we look at the jubilee institution rooted in Israel's theology and practice of land tenure, we will see how these different angles and levels of interpretation work. The year of jubilee ended a seven-year cycle of sabbaticals. Leviticus 25:10 says, 'Consecrate the fiftieth year and pro-claim liberty throughout the land to all its inhabitants. It shall be a jubilee for you; each one of you is to return to his family property and each to his own clan.' Those who were enslaved because of debt would be released, and land sold because of economic need would be restored to the original family. Detailed instructions regarding the jubilee and its relationship to redeeming land and those sold into slavery are found in Leviticus 25—27. In essence, the jubilee was concerned with the family and the land, and was rooted in the social structure of Israelite kinship, the economic system of land tenure and the theological scope of Israel's faith.

In Judges, Gideon's response to his angelic visitor refers to the three tiers of the tribe, the clan and the household, which made up Israelite kinship (Judges 6:15). The household and the clan were of greater importance both socially and economically than the tribe. The household was a place of authority, security and protection. The clan was a group of households that were named after the grandsons of Jacob or attached to a territorial area (Numbers 26; 1 Chronicles 4—8). The clan comprised both kinship and territory and was responsible for preserving the land given to each household. While the jubilee was intended to protect the smaller household, it also served to establish an economic practice for redeeming the land and the people.

A system of land tenure operated on the basis of the kinship units, and the land was given to tribes 'according to their clans' (Joshua 13—21). In Israel the land was wholly owned by the households according to their needs. To protect the system of kinship distribution, the land could not be bought and sold as a commercial asset, but was to remain within the household or extended family.

'The land shall not be sold permanently, for the land belongs to me; for you are "guests" and "residents" with me' (Leviticus 25:23, my translation). This verse at the core of Leviticus 25 reveals one of the central pillars of the faith of Israel. The land inhabited by Israel belonged to the Lord. It had been promised and given to Israel and was their inheritance as God's chosen people. Israelites are described in Leviticus as guests and residents, aliens and tenants of the Lord. The Lord was the supreme landlord and Israel was his collective tenant, but there were also a class of people with no stake in the tenure of the land, who were guests/aliens, perhaps not ethnic Israelites. They too lived in a relationship of protected dependency on God. The outworking of this model for Israelites in relation to God was egalitarian. The indebted brother was to be treated with compassion, justice and generosity, just as God treated all Israel. The exodus is regarded as the act of redemption in which God bought Israel for himself. All were now slaves of God, and those slaves whom God has freed cannot make slaves of one another (Leviticus 25:39, 42).

The first few verses of Leviticus 25 outline the law given to Moses for the sabbatical year of the land: 'In the seventh year the land is to have a sabbath of rest, a sabbath to the Lord' (v. 4). It is a rest from cultivation, although the kinspeople can eat whatever the land produces naturally. The fiftieth year is to be consecrated and liberty for all declared. It will be a jubilee in which everyone returns to his own property. This is a liberty from the burden of debt and a return to the ancestral property. It was these two elements of the jubilee that were taken up by the prophets and New Testament writers.

The cost of a piece of land was determined by the number of years left before the next jubilee year. In effect, the purchaser was leasing the land and buying the number of harvests remaining until the jubilee restored the land to the original owner. Special inducements in the form of blessings were promised for observance of the sabbatical regulations, which hinged on the theological principle that obedience required faith in the Lord's providence.

The two main differences between redemption and jubilee provisions are, first, the timing and, second, the goal. Redemption was a duty that was exercised at any time as situations required, whereas jubilee took place twice a century and involved the whole nation. The goal of redemption was to preserve the land and the clan members, whereas the goal of the jubilee was to preserve the household. The jubilee was thus a mechanism to prevent inequality within the clans and to preserve the socio-economic fabric of multiple-household land tenure.

When we explore the jubilee from a typological approach, we see that Jesus took up the institution of jubilee and applied it to the age of fulfilment that he inaugurated. He claimed that the hopes of restoration and messianic reversal were being fulfilled in his own ministry. Jesus' clearest statement of this appears in the 'Nazareth manifesto', where he quotes directly from Isaiah 61, which is heavily influenced by jubilee concepts (Luke 4:16–30).

In Acts, Peter takes up the core of the jubilee hope and applies it to the restoration of the whole of creation, not just restoration of the land to the farmer. The early Church responded to this hope and applied it to a mutual economic help that fulfilled the sabbatical hopes of Deuteronomy: 'There will be no needy person among you' (Acts 4:34). In following the Messiah, the believers' lives were filled with the Spirit and echoed the fulfilment of the jubilee hope and its sabbatical institutions.

When we consider how Israel's paradigm speaks to the whole of humanity, it is helpful to move around three angles: the economic, social and theological angles. Israel's model of jubilee can be interpreted economically as a universal moral principle on the basis of the moral consistency of God. The jubilee existed to protect a form of equal land tenure and to prevent inequality of wealth and land ownership in society. It mirrors the creation principle that the earth is given by God to humans, who live as co-stewards of its resources. This principle is affirmed in Leviticus 25:23, in respect of Israel, that 'the land is mine', and in Psalm 24:1, in respect of all humanity, that 'the earth is the Lord's, and everything in it, the world, and all who live in it'.

The jubilee was not a handout of charity, but an opportunity to rebuild and restore family units to enable them to provide for themselves again. This requires very creative thinking if we are to apply it to our own situation. What resources and opportunities would we need to enable people to be self-sufficient and to enjoy the dignity of all that self provision entails?[3]

In a social context, jubilee exemplifies a concern for the family unit, through moral and legislative means. Its aim was to restore the dignity and economic viability of the family units so that each could participate in society. Debt is recognized in the Old Testament as the cause of many social ills, but the jubilee was a way of limiting the social consequences of debt: the economic collapse of one generation could be restored by another, thereby releasing a family from perpetual bondage to debt. It is not hard to see how this principle could be applied today on a much larger scale, involving national debts of poor countries.

At the same time, the jubilee theologically proclaims the sovereignty of God over time and nature. Obedience to the jubilee would require obedience to God. This makes the year holy, 'a sabbath to the Lord' (Leviticus 25:4), observed out of the fear of the Lord (v. 17). It also requires faith in the providence of God and the experience of God's forgiveness. In order to apply the jubilee model, it would be necessary for people to understand these principles and to know the redeeming action of God, to know God's justice and be prepared to put their hope in his promises: 'The wholeness of the jubilee model embraces the church's evangelistic mission, its personal and social ethics and its hope.'[4]

Finally, our interpretation of jubilee must integrate with future hope. The economic aspects of liberty and restoration become terms of hope and longing for the future in the wider metaphorical application of jubilee. The weak and oppressed are a main focus of the mission of the Servant of the Lord in Isaiah 58 and 61. Liberation for the oppressed is put along-side a transformation of nature (Isaiah 35). These passages integrate the personal, social, economic, political, international and spiritual realms. Our use of the jubilee today must preserve that balance and integration, enabling us to play our part in what God will ultimately join together. The future hope is for a glorious jubilee celebration.

Then I saw a new heaven and a new earth, for the first heaven and the first earth had passed away, and there was no longer any sea. I saw the Holy City, the new Jerusalem, coming down out of heaven from God, prepared as a bride beautifully dressed for her husband. And I heard a loud voice from the throne saying, 'Now the dwelling of God is with men, and he will live with them… He will wipe every tear from their eyes. There will be no more death or mourning or crying or pain, for the old order of things has passed away.' He who was seated on the throne said, 'I am making everything new!' Then he said, 'Write this down, for these words are trustworthy and true.'

REVELATION 21:1–5

❖

CAN THERE BE A SABBATH
FOR MARSHLAND?

Karin Boisclair-Joly, A Rocha France

The Vallée des Baux, near Arles, in Provence, is part of the flood basin of the powerful Rhône river. Historically, it held vast marshes, which were drained over time by the Romans, the monks of the local abbey and, more recently, farmers. To the north, the valley is bordered by limestone hills, which, in torrential autumnal rains, also hurl water into the canals that supply the needs of this fertile agricultural area. Les Tourades, the home of A Rocha in France, is seated on the valley floor, within flood-reach of the waters from rice paddies-turned-private nature reserve. The A Rocha team is as much concerned about the risk of extreme floods as any of the landowners with whom they partner for the conservation of special species and places in the valley.

Several kilometres to the east, the lowest part of the valley contains an especially rich biodiversity of plants, insects, amphibians and birds. This was formerly the Étang du Comte, which encompassed 1800 hectares. Now mostly dry, it is divided between twelve landowners, three of whom own the lion's share. Of these, M. and Mme Donadieu hold the Ilon marsh, the only remnant of the Étang du Comte. Early in A Rocha's development, and still extremely important for the association's credibility in the valley, an agreement with the Donadieus provided a key entry-point into the complicated social landscape that informs local land use. The Ilon had been managed for 40 years from the perspective that while the land must work for its keep—hosting olive groves, grazing, hunting, fishing, farming and apiculture—it is also a haven for wildlife, to be warded carefully. Some pressures, like that of development for holiday mansions and greenhouses, can be resisted, but others cannot: today, the Ilon experiences reduced water quality because the canal that feeds the marsh drains an area of intensive agriculture. Although their careful attitude has been good for the land and its creatures, there has been a cost to the owners: they have isolated themselves; they are weary and anticipate defeat.

In 2003, A Rocha's gaze turned towards the Ilon's neighbours. We wondered what the attitudes were of the landowners towards the magnificent natural heritage embodied in the Étang du Comte. Happily, the two other principal *proprietaires* welcomed contact with A Rocha and the opportunity it offered to acquaint them with the wildlife on their land; they invited basic inventories and regular monitoring. One landowner is enthusiastic about the idea of a management strategy that encourages wildlife, and the other has asked for A Rocha's help as she explores a major practical and conceptual shift in the use of her land.

Mas Malaga is a beautiful estate with orchards, meadows dotted with bulls raised for *tauromachie*, and reed-bordered fields that burgeon with corn—a highly subsidized crop that places a heavy strain on the earth in which it grows. Malaga is the end-recipient of various problems upstream, results of the valley's system of canals and dykes that badly need rethinking and rebuilding rather than repair. Increasingly heavy periodic flooding, like that of autumn 2003, not only destroys the crops but is also very costly to pump away, both financially and environmentally. The owner's frustration with canal authorities and the local government runs high.

What alternatives does Mas Malaga's owner have? A Rocha's relationship with her began as she and her family considered returning the corn fields to a marshland state on which they can offer private hunting rights as a means for the land to pay for itself. With A Rocha's encouragement, she is now considering the benefits of eco-tourism for her land, family, employees and the municipality itself. In exploring how to honour the intrinsic value of her land and its potential to host masses of wildlife, she has established relations with the other two major owners of the Étang du Comte to find out about their attitudes and hopes for their land.

It is a privilege for A Rocha team members to participate in the gradual evolution of attitudes and behaviours towards wildlife in the Vallée des Baux. The team have particularly noticed the healing that has occurred through people's increased interaction with the natural landscape. Now when people stop to consider the landscape and the marvellous creatures living around them, they become more relaxed. They are refreshed by the beauty and variety of the scenery before them. The Étang du Comte, despite its degraded and fragile state, is restoring relationships between neighbours. A corn field is sounding a wake-up call to its owners to reconsider their expectations of the land. Will there be a year of jubilee for the Étang du Comte? As A Rocha and its neighbours in the Vallée des Baux consider habitat restoration, they also consider relationship restoration—between people, between the land and its caretakers, and ultimately, we hope, between the creation and its creator.

WISDOM

Ghillean Prance

Wisdom is strongly linked to creation in a number of biblical passages. In Proverbs 8, Wisdom is personified as a woman appealing to people to follow righteousness rather than the destructive ways of the foolish. This is followed by a statement of Wisdom's role in creation:

The Lord brought me forth as the first of his works,
before his deeds of old;
I was appointed from eternity,
from the beginning, before the world began.
When there were no oceans, I was given birth,
when there were no springs abounding with water;
before the mountains were settled in place,
before the hills, I was given birth,
before he made the earth or its fields
or any of the dust of the world.
I was there when he set the heavens in place,
when he marked out the horizon on the face of the deep,
when he established the clouds above
and fixed securely the fountains of the deep,
when he gave the sea its boundary
so the waters would not overstep his command,
and when he marked out the foundations of the earth.
Then I was the craftsman at his side.
I was filled with delight day after day,
rejoicing always in his presence,
rejoicing in his whole world
and delighting in mankind.

Now then, my sons, listen to me;
blessed are those who keep my ways.
PROVERBS 8:22–32

In some places this has been interpreted Christologically, for we know that Christ took part in creation: 'He [Christ] is the image of the invisible God, the firstborn of all creation; for in him all things in heaven and on earth were created, things visible and invisible, whether thrones or dominions or rulers or powers—all things were created through him and for him' (Colossians 1:15–16, NRSV). The Holy Spirit is sometimes thought of as the female aspect of God, and we know that in the beginning of creation 'The Spirit of God was moving over the face of the waters' (Genesis 1:2, RSV).

Wisdom in Proverbs 8 is representing the feminine creative and ordering role of God. Wisdom outlines the progressive, step-by-step creation of the physical world (vv. 24–29), echoing the Genesis accounts of creation, and was beside the Lord 'like a master worker' (v. 30a, NRSV). She rejoiced about the progress of creation and as a result was 'daily God's delight' (v. 30b, NRSV). The rejoicing included delight that the end result of creation was a place for humankind to inhabit (v. 31).

The last verses (vv. 32–36) are an appeal to listen and follow Wisdom, 'for whoever who finds me finds life' (v. 35). It is interesting that this chapter on Wisdom brings together creation and righteous behaviour. If Wisdom's ways had been followed, then creation would not be in the situation it is in now as a result of the destructive nature of fallen humankind. Wisdom calls us to 'take my instruction instead of silver, and knowledge rather than choice gold' (v. 10, NRSV). It is greed and materialism that are destroying God's creation today. Wisdom must be mourning rather than rejoicing over the present state of creation at the beginning of the third millennium.

JOB 12:7-12

In Job 12:7–12, we can find an insight into the understanding and knowledge of Job even when he was suffering greatly and enduring the accusations of Zophar and his other false comforters. Job had a well-integrated view of creation from which he had learned much:

But ask the animals, and they will teach you,
or the birds of the air, and they will tell you;
or speak to the earth, and it will teach you,
or let the fish of the sea inform you;
Which of all these does not know
that the hand of the Lord has done this?
In his hand is the life of every creature
and the breath of all mankind.
Does not the ear test words
as the tongue tastes food?
Is not wisdom found among the aged?
Does not long life bring understanding?

Job was someone who learned not only from the word of God but also from the works of God. He saw that the birds, beasts, plants and fish were all the handiwork of God, that they declare his glory. Job is arguing back to his persecutors through his deep knowledge and love of both the creator and his creation. This is surely true wisdom, as opposed to all the verbiage of his friends.

Throughout Job's discourses to his friends, he uses examples from his intimate knowledge of creation. Reading through Job's answers, one cannot but be impressed by his considerable knowledge of wild animals, plants and the physical universe. Job 28:12–28 reveals his attitude to wisdom, when he acknowledges that ultimate wisdom is known only to God, while at the same time he urges all to seek wisdom: 'And he said to man, "The fear of the Lord—that is wisdom, and to shun evil is understanding"' (v. 28).

It is therefore not surprising that, when God finally answers Job out of the whirlwind (38:1), we have the most wonderful description of the marvels of creation in the whole Bible. One might have expected God to answer Job with a call to repentance, but instead God builds upon Job's wisdom. Here we have an interpretation of the goodness of creation that God saw in Genesis as each stage was completed. God begins with the physical side—the stars, the sea, light, rain, snow, ice and thunder—and continues with a fine lesson on the natural history of the Middle East. In chapters 38 and 39 we learn about the hunting habits of lions, eagles and ravens, the calving and feeding of young deer, the ostrich that does not sit on her eggs, the bravery of horses, the soaring of the hawk and how the eagles feed their young.

Chapter 41 continues with a description of the monster Leviathan, the crocodile, and of Behemoth, the hippopotamus. These two creatures represented sheer strength, power and wildness that people of Job's day were unable to control. The lesson from these chapters of Job is the greatness of God's creative power in comparison to the inferior ability of humans. Did Job make these wonders? Can he tame them? Wisdom is to fear and respect God, and folly is to claim equality with God. Ultimately, Job is humbled by the greatness of creation.

What emerges from this part of the scriptures for me is the lesson that we can learn much of God and his ways from the study of the marvels of his creation, whether we look at the stars in heaven or the plants and birds around us. However, we live in a time of environmental crisis when creation is being destroyed or, at the very least, seriously threatened through pollution of the atmosphere, the rivers, seas and land, through the loss of biological species, the destruction of forests and the loss of that most precious resource, soil. Evil is triumphing over goodness at present.

These chapters on wisdom from the books of Proverbs and Job are a call to return to respect for nature and for all creation. We are not to worship creation but to become better stewards of it, because it is God's creation in which he takes a great pride. Job understood that 'God saw that it was good' (Genesis 1:21). A God who looks at nature and sees it as good, and also uses it to humble Job, is a God who is interested in far more than humanity. This is a God who loves all living things in their diversity. Jesus also reminded us that even the sparrows are important to God, and told us, 'Look at the birds of the air: they neither sow nor reap nor gather into barns, and yet your heavenly Father feeds them' (Matthew 6:26, RSV).

This discourse to Job should not be thought of as an address to him alone. It is in the scriptures to remind us all of God the creator and of the goodness and greatness of his creation; to remind us and to challenge us to join with God in wonderment at creation, but also to be stewards until Christ returns. That is true wisdom.

The pathway to this wisdom was given to us by James: 'If any of you is lacking in wisdom, ask God, who gives to all generously and ungrudgingly, and it will be given you. But ask in faith, never doubting, for the one who doubts is like a wave of the sea, driven and tossed by the wind' (James 1:5–6a, NRSV).

The fear of the Lord that is wisdom is the first step to creation care. If that is so, then those who fear the Lord have a great responsibility not to be complacent while creation around us is destroyed, but to be leaders in its stewardship. Wisdom has been lacking in much of the Church. The unity of wisdom and creation in the Bible should be a challenge to us, just as it was to Job. There is a choice that we have to make between good and evil, between wisdom and folly, and ultimately between God and Satan. The right choices will lead us into creation care rather than its destruction. The apostle Paul made it clear that the testimony of creation leaves us with no excuse for disbelief: 'Ever since the creation of the world his invisible nature, namely, his eternal power and deity, has been clearly perceived in the things that have been made. So they are without excuse' (Romans 1:20, RSV). It also leaves us with no excuse for avoiding our Christian responsibility for creation.

THE A ROCHA CZECH FIELD STUDY CENTRE

Pavel Svetlik, A Rocha Czech Republic
(translated by Anna Novakova)

An old building, a former textile factory, was recently purchased for the future work of A Rocha Czech Republic. The building had originally been an old barley mill, its Czech name *Na Krupárne* speaking of the mill's original function.

The mill is without a turbine now, but the water of the *Zlaty potok*, the Golden Stream, runs through the house just as it always used to when it was a working mill. Despite all the changes in ownership over the years, the house has one permanent and well-loved resident: the dipper. It has made its home in the so-called 'refrigerator', the place where the water wheel and later the turbine used to be.

Ever since my childhood I've been fascinated by the dipper. This beautiful bird has influenced my interest in the natural world. The nimble dipper loves clean, cold, flowing water. In hard winters, when the water is frozen over, the dipper will skilfully move through cracks in the ice and dive to the bottom of the stream to find its favourite food—caddis fly larvae and other underwater insects.

Over the last few years, the dipper population on the Golden Stream has decreased significantly. Recent huge floods have stripped away the rich food resources from the streams and riverbeds, while at the same time the natural nesting habitat for the dipper has diminished; both of these factors have had a great influence on the dipper's decline. The A Rocha project monitors the diminishing population curve of this increasingly rare bird and has committed itself to work to reverse the negative trend. By providing nest boxes, and platforms on the water's edge, we are trying to support the remaining dipper population. Small and cheap improvements like these, especially on the bridges and buildings on the banks of rivers, are often enough to help stabilize the population.

The dipper, in Czech also nicknamed 'the water blackbird' or 'the mill blackbird', has actually nested in our A Rocha building for decades. For that purpose, it chose a special niche in the wall, high above the water level. When the mill was fully operational, the axis of the water wheel was probably positioned in about the same place. Nowadays, it is wonderfully hidden from humans as well as from other predators, and a young brood fledges twice a year in that nest. The water wheel itself disappeared from *Krupárné* many years ago, but the wheel of the course of nature keeps turning around. Sometimes its turning can be rather rough and merciless, particularly towards God's creation.

A Rocha Czech Republic's field study centre is at a very early stage, still in the throes of being born. We know that we have many challenges and adventures ahead of us, but the good news is that there is one living resident in our very dilapidated centre: our old-new neighbour, the dipper. This marvellous work of God, a jewel in nature, this lover of clean flowing water, is both a promise and a challenge to us: to wait for the streams of God's water, for blessing. Just as Francis of Assisi spoke to God's creatures, so we could say, 'Little dipper, dear brother, we are looking forward to being with you, to being friends with you in the future. We want to be a help to you and to your endangered family. May that old mill continue to be a good home to you.'

CREATION AND THE GOSPELS

Peter Carruthers

Beginnings are always significant. My early interest in agriculture took me first to the account of Jesus walking with his disciples in the grain fields one Sabbath (Matthew 12:1). This prompted me to ask whether or not there were any specific 'creation connections' at Jesus' birth and at the start of his ministry. There were! While the Gospels have not traditionally been the first resort for a theology of the creation or principles for environmental responsibility, there is much to be gleaned from the life and words of Jesus. I have sought to understand all these passages from a creation and environment viewpoint. It goes without saying that this is not their only meaning.

The objection voiced by the Pharisees, as Jesus' disciples picked grain, was just one of six disputes recorded in the Gospels between Jesus and the Pharisees, relating to Sabbath observance. The others concerned healing. In the dispute about picking grains on the Sabbath day, the focus is on the land, and this short account opens up to the reader a wealth of biblical principles for farming and food production.

In the Ten Commandments given to Moses by God at Mount Sinai, the Sabbath day was instituted as a day of rest—for families, workers and livestock (Exodus 20:8–11). Essentially, the legitimate work of tending the land and other labour for six days of the week was to cease on the seventh day. This command echoed the pattern of God's own work of creation. The Sabbath day anticipated the Sabbath year, when slaves were freed (Exodus 21:1–11), debts were cancelled (Deuteronomy 15:1–11) and the land rested (Leviticus 25:1–7). Both anticipated the year of jubilee (Leviticus 25:8–55), a Sabbath of Sabbaths, in which, in addition to all the provisions of the Sabbath year, everyone was to 'return to his property and… to his family' (v. 10, RSV). The jubilee, in effect, placed strict limits on the growth of private wealth, as land could not be sold permanently.

Sabbath and jubilee protected and liberated the oppressed, those without a voice and without power—servants, the poor, domestic animals and the land itself. Indeed, quoting directly from Isaiah 61, Jesus inaugurated his public ministry in the 'Nazareth Manifesto' by declaring himself the fulfilment of the jubilee institution, the year of the Lord's favour (Luke 4:16–21). And in the grain field story he drives the same point home, stating, 'I desire mercy, not sacrifice' (Matthew 12:7).

As Jesus says, the disciples were guiltless. Picking the grain by hand was acceptable (Deuteronomy 23:25), and their doing so on the Sabbath was a breach of rabbinic law, not biblical law.[1] In total contrast to the legalistic bondage of the Pharisees' Sabbath, Jesus proclaimed the Sabbath as a festival of freedom—both for people and the earth.

Sabbath and jubilee give us three principles for farming and food production.

- Sharing—with the poor.[2]
- Caring—for the earth.
- Restraint—of power and wealth.[3]

Of these three, 'sharing' is most explicit in the story. The disciples are representative of (if not in actuality) the poor and hungry, with whom the good fruits of the earth should be shared. It is interesting that Luke's account suggests that the grain was barley, the food of the poor, rather than wheat.[4]

The principle of caring for the earth is also present, although perhaps less explicit. The Son of Man who descended from Adam, made from the dust of the earth (Genesis 2:7), is also Lord of the earth (Daniel 7:13; Hebrews 1:3), that is to say, 'one greater than the temple' (Matthew 12:6; Hebrews 9:11–28), and Lord of the Sabbath (Luke 6:5), the 'Lord of mercy'— a mercy that, as the psalmist says, is over *all* his works (Psalm 145:9).

It is well known that there are huge disparities across the world between those who have a surfeit of food and those who go hungry. Added to this is a growing awareness of the impact of modern industrial agriculture on the environment.[5] There are also enormous imbalances in the world food system: a diminishing share of consumers' expenditure reaches producers, and oligopolies of powerful buyers range against thousands of 'must sell' sellers.[6] Against the above three biblical principles, global farming is 'weighed in the balances and found wanting' (Daniel 5:27, RSV). Instead of keeping the Sabbath, we have created, as Breuggemann put it, a 'Sabbath less society'.[7]

Nevertheless, at the heart of the grain fields story is a message of hope. Both the Sabbath and jubilee anticipate the messianic age. The Sabbath institution both looks back to the rest of creation and forward to its liberation.[8] And a central part of that vision is of a transformed agriculture, 'when the ploughman shall overtake the reaper' (Amos 9:13, ESV), a world in which 'they shall sit every man under his vine and under his fig tree' (Micah 4:4, ESV).

The proclamation of the messianic age is also in focus in Luke's account of Jesus' birth (Luke 2:8–14). Heaven breaks open and angels announce peace on earth to shepherds protecting their lambs, including, presumably, from wolves. To them, 'peace' might mean a 'world where you didn't have to live out in the fields in the depth of winter, and at the dead of night looking after sheep and protecting young lambs from ravenous wolves',[9] a world, as in Isaiah's vision of that age to come, where 'the wolf and the lamb shall graze together' (Isaiah 65:25, ESV).

With the announcement of peace is the announcement of a 'sign'—a baby lying in an animal feeding trough. Jesus is born close to the animals, and his first visitors are a group of pastoralists. Echlin imaginatively re-constructs the life of Jesus in Nazareth as one that continued to be lived close to animals, farming and the land, arguing that this is why he used analogies from agriculture in his teaching, more than analogies from the workshop.[10] As the promised Messiah, Jesus inaugurates the promised age of peace on earth. This includes not only peace among people, but also with the animals and within the whole created order (Isaiah 11:1–9; 65:17–25).

While the picture of the shepherds protecting their livestock is indicative of the disharmony within a fallen creation, it is at the same time evocative of Adam's original calling to tend and protect the garden (Genesis 2:15). Jesus, the 'last Adam' (1 Corinthians 15:45), restores what the first Adam lost, making it possible for people and the earth to fulfil their original destiny.

Heaven breaks open again at Jesus' baptism, in a trinitarian epiphany (Mark 1:9–11). Jesus' immersion in water is symbolic of his solidarity with humanity and with the earth itself. It is evocative of the flood—the judgment and cleansing the earth by water—and of Jonah, whose actual or metaphorical death and resurrection in the waters of the sea were the 'means of grace' to those destined for judgment. Just as the salvation of Nineveh's people was extended to their livestock (Jonah 4:11), so the salvation achieved by Jesus will extend to the whole of creation.

The Spirit hovering over the water, recalling the first creation (Genesis 1:2), announces the new creation. His descending on Jesus recalls the Spirit of Lord resting on the 'shoot… from the stump of Jesse' (Isaiah 11:1–2), and signifies the realization of the peaceable kingdom (Isaiah 11:6–9).

The Father's words, echoing Psalm 2:7, proclaim Jesus as king. As Echlin notes, 'This is ecologically significant because, in Jewish hopes, good kings ensure good weather, ample rain and fertile soil (Psalm 72:3, 6,16).'[11]

In the wilderness temptation that follows, we see Jesus 'with the wild animals' (Mark 1:13). The sense here is of close association and friendship,[12] solidarity and fellowship.[13] The last Adam, the one who brings peace, is enjoying companionship with the animals as at the beginning in Eden. By doing so, he again declares the coming of the kingdom of God 'on earth as it is in heaven' and himself as Messiah and king.

The Gospels describe, or refer to, eight of Jesus' appearances after his resurrection. Both the geographical locations and the physical content alert us to their relevance for the earth. Apart from two in the upper room, or in undefined places, these appearances are in a garden (John 20:11–18), on a country road (Luke 24:13–35), on a mountain (Matthew 28:16), by a lake (John 21:1–25) and, finally, on the Mount of Olives (Luke 24:50–53; Acts 1:4–12). Food features in three: Jesus breaks bread at Emmaus, eats fish and honeycomb in the upper room, and cooks breakfast by the Sea of Galilee.

'SUPPOSING HIM TO BE THE GARDENER' (JOHN 20:1–18, NRSV)

Mark reports simply that when Jesus rose 'he appeared first to Mary Magdalene, from whom he had cast seven demons' (Mark 16:9, ESV). John gives more detail. Mary hangs back after the others had seen the empty tomb, and encounters Jesus in the garden, believing him at first to be the gardener.

It is significant that this first appearance took place in a garden, that it was to a woman, and that she mistook him for the gardener. The garden speaks of Eden, the place of cooperation between God and humanity in tending and caring for creation. It is fitting that Jesus walking in the garden, like God in Eden, comes first to Mary, representing as it were womankind, declaring that what Eve lost he has recovered. It is fitting also that she mistakes him for the gardener, for he is! In his depiction of this encounter, the 15th-century painter Fra Angelico painted Jesus with a hoe to emphasize this point.[14]

In the place where Jesus was crucified there was a garden and in the garden a new tomb. From that tomb the New Man rose, lifting from its bondage the whole body of things as well as of men. True Nature was re-established. Man in Christ is made heir once more of a new earth. No wonder Mary, on the Resurrection morning thought he was the gardener for indeed he was—the new Adam and the New Man; the restored cooperation.

LORD MACLEOD OF FUINARY[15]

THE ROAD TO EMMAUS (LUKE 24:13–34)

Later on resurrection day, Jesus appears to two disciples on the road to Emmaus. Like Mary Magdalene, they do not, at first, recognize him. In her case, all that was needed was for Jesus to speak her name. For Cleopas and companion, recognition only came when Jesus 'took bread, blessed and broke it, and gave it to them' (v. 30, NRSV).

Just as in the meeting of Jesus and Mary in the garden, there are echoes of Eden in the Emmaus story. As Adam and Eve's eyes were opened (Genesis 3:7), so were the eyes of the two opened—not to guilt and shame, but to the one who had redeemed what the first man and woman lost, and who makes all things new.

As one concerned with the countryside and farming, I like to think of Jesus walking through the fields, flocks and forests of the Judean countryside, silently declaring the message of redemption, now made possible by his death and resurrection, to a creation waiting 'with eager longing' (Romans 8:19, NRSV). But the main message for the earth in the Emmaus account is found in the matter of continuity and transformation.

Jesus was the same, yet different; continuous, but transformed. They recognized him, yet they did not. He was expected, yet unexpected. Their *hearts* burned within them (v. 32) on first meeting, but only later were their *eyes opened* (v. 31). In his vivid portrayal of the moment of recognition, the 17th-century painter Michelangelo Merisi da Caravaggio drew out this reality by breaking with the convention of the time and painting Jesus without a beard.[16]

Paul makes it clear that those who 'belong to Christ' (1 Corinthians 15:23, NRSV) will also be raised as he was raised, with a transformed body 'like his glorious body' (Philippians 3:21). And this continuity and transformation extends to the earth itself. For Jesus' death and resurrection inaugurated a process that culminates in the liberation and transformation of the whole of creation (Romans 8:21), in 'new heavens and a new earth' (2 Peter 3:13, NRSV).

BY THE LAKESIDE (JOHN 21:1-14)

The third appearance takes us back to where our brief journey through the Gospels began. This is the second miraculous draft of fish recorded in the Gospels. Both took place after a fruitless night's fishing; both were defining moments for Simon Peter. The first (Luke 5:1–11) preceded his call, the second his reinstatement. There was one essential difference, however: on the post-resurrection occasion, the nets did not break.

Like the feeding of the four and five thousand, the catch of 153 big fish promises and 'foreshadows the flowering of God's creatures in God's kingdom',[17] the super-abundance that will mark the time 'when the ploughman shall overtake the reaper and the treader of grapes him who sows the seed; the mountains shall drip sweet wine, and all the hills shall flow with it' (Amos 9:13, ESV); when, in William Dix's words based on Psalm 65, 'Bright robes of gold the fields adorn, the hills with joy are ringing, The valleys stand so thick with corn that even they are singing'.

❖

'SEE HOW THE LILIES OF THE FIELD GROW'

Will Simonson, A Rocha Portugal

'See how the lilies of the field grow,' Jesus is recorded saying in Matthew's Gospel (6:28). From my earliest visits as a young botanist to the Ria De Alvor, there is one plant that has always stood out for me: the sea squill *Urginea maritima*, the lily of the end-of-summer Algarvian field.

My first field project for A Rocha, under the direction of Dr Bob Pullan, the Trust's founding chairman, was to survey and map the coastal scrublands of the Quinta da Rocha headlands, one of A Rocha's first forays into botany. It was in September 1988, and the fields were turning sandy brown, crisp-dry, and the air was still hot with the scent of fennel and other aromatic plants. There were few wildflowers to be seen, but nevertheless I enjoyed mapping the evergreen vegetation of the mastic tree, the holly oak, and rock-roses. At the same time, I first discovered, rising out of the ground between the clearings, the vigorous leafless spikes of the sea squill.

The sea squill can be found on the coasts and even interior regions of Portugal and the Mediterranean region, where the annual summer drought creates the dry stage for the squill's flowering finale. The flowering spikes have a waxy violet hue, and reach the height of a child. Each one bears a dense raceme of, say, 200 white flowers, opening in a Mexican wave towards the top. The individual flowers are perfect stars of David, no more than a centimetre across, six white petals each with a central vein of purple or green, enclosing six lime-green stamens on white anthers, and a central yellow female part. This flowering profusion arises out of a baked earth, but a little excavation reveals where such energy comes from: a bulb lying just below the surface, perhaps the size and weight of a large onion. From the same spot, long strap-like leaves appear in the winter, once the flowering stem is itself a dry stalk, and persist to the following summer, recharging the bulb of its spent reserves.

Ever since my first encounter with this species, I have found it evocative of that time when the summer heat is about to burn itself out. The sea squill is, for me, the John the Baptist of the plant world, heralding the new life that is to come with the arrival of the autumn rains later in September. Not that the rains themselves are the trigger for its growth: it is an action of faith and expectation rather than response. Neither is its light of pronouncement placed under a bushel, but rather it is in the rocky spaces between the bushes that the proud plants are to be found. Perhaps there is a challenge here, to stand out, stand tall and be a symbol of hope and the coming of green pastures.

FURTHER READING

C.J.H. Wright, *Living as the People of God* (IVP, 1983).

CREATION AND INCARNATION

James Houston

The Czech novelist Milan Kundera entitled one of his novels *The Unbearable Lightness of Being* to describe the existential emptiness of postmodern living. It is a Kafkaesque emptiness that lost the sense of reality once the heavy-booted totalitarian ideology of Marxism disappeared from the radar screen.

A visit to Prague today will demonstrate this reaction in a twofold way. The drab greyness typical of a Communist city has been replaced by an infinite variety of pastel colours to represent the medieval facades of what are still fine historic buildings. Then there is also the explosion of the human spirit in the vulgarity of pornography. Both are reactions to oppression, yet both no longer have a meaning beyond the economic pragmatism of tourism and voyeurism. Likewise, it seems that God has slowly been displaced from his creation to permit his humanly conceived rival, Mother Nature, to reign, so that all the order of universal values, distinguishing good from evil, are disappearing, to be substituted by Nature's fearsome ambiguity.

The difference between these two perceptions is that while God is the creator of all things, humanity is the inventor of Nature. Thus, to take the thinking self as the naturalistic basis of all things is to face the universe heroically alone. No wonder some scientists are looking for signs of other intelligence in outer space, to bring some cheer to what Loren Eisley has called the plight of secular man as 'the cosmic orphan'.[1]

The philosopher Edmund Husserl, three years before his death in 1938, gave his celebrated lectures on the crisis of European humanity, by which he really meant the moral crisis of all Western civilization. The crisis for him lay at the beginning of the modern era, in Galileo and Descartes, when the one-sided investigative nature of modern science began. This was when the reduction of the world to a mere object of technical and mathematical investigation first began. It has interrogated the world ever since, seized by the passion 'to know', for the sake of more 'knowledge', more power. The more the scientist now 'knows', the more the tunnel vision of specialized disciplines has grown too, and so the less clear the world as a whole, or his own self, has become. It has plunged further into what Husserl's pupil Heidegger called 'the forgetting of being'—dimming the meaning of reality.

The structure of reality consists of many grades, of which each pre-supposes those lower as well as higher than itself. They may broadly be conceived of as matter, life, mind, and spirit. Each has many grades within itself, but in each case the lower cannot explain the higher. Matter can be understood by physics and chemistry, as life can be understood by biology and genetics, but life gives new meaning to matter, as mind can add further meanings to life. So, too, mind as intellect requires spirit to guide it in reaching higher realities, such as motive, value, and human benefit. As William Temple pointed out:

The only explanation of the Universe that would really explain it all, in the sense of providing an answer to the question why it exists and raising no further questions, would be the demonstration that it is the creation of a Will which is the creative act that seeks an intelligible good. But that is Theism and theism of some kind is the only theory of the universe which could really explain it.[2]

If theism is viewed as untenable, then the universe becomes inexplicable. Thus the final issue can only be: what kind of theism is untenable, and which is not?

CREATION CAN BE ACCEPTABLE ONLY THROUGH CREATURELINESS

One response has been that we can no longer afford to remain detached observers of our cosmos, because of the increasing gravity of our environmental crisis. Instead of standing over our planet, we need to live in unity within our planet, in some kind of 'panentheism', or indeed some modified form of pantheism. This would designate a way of looking at all life—divine, human, biological and physical—as inextricably an inter-woven, 'synchronous' pattern. Matthew Fox would thus revise the whole biblical framework of the doctrine of creation, in an advocacy of a new 'nature spirituality' that he naively assumes will put 'mankind back into nature'.[3] He forgets that if humankind has such powers over nature as the environmental crisis seems to assess, then such a monistic response will only further reduce human responsibility from being capable of taking some remedial action.

The feminist response of Rosemary Ruether is more sophisticated, in associating the Hebrew myth of creation as in counterpoise to the Babylon and Canaanite mythologies of creation. For the latter, 'creation' is interpreted as a movement of self-regulation within a single continuum, that is 'the matrix of creation-chaos'.[4] For the Hebrews, however, she interprets them to affirm that the creator is more like an artisan working on material outside his own nature, by 'word-act', shaping from 'above', with a mandate for the male to rule over it and assert his dominion. As Lynn White asked in a famous essay of 1973, is the biblical mandate to 'have dominion' not the primary cause of the environment crisis today?[5] So, too, Ruether also advocates a recovery of balance and harmony between humanity and nature, which would deny any sovereignty to the creator.

Images of God asserting cultural power are also condemned by Sallie McFague, who would prefer more biological concepts of creation as 'God's body', again wholly in conflict with the biblical narrative of 'creation by the Word'.[6] The bogey of so-called 'biblical patriarchialism' is never far away from these feminist reactions, for there are fundamental sources of muddled thinking about God as some kind of bigoted male chauvinist when speaking of him as the creator of all things. Actually, there should be, much more realistically, a reaction to Aristotle's interpretation of the female as only a half-formed male, than to the biblical narrative of male–female complement.[7] 'Human dominion' over the created order should also be interpreted more responsibly as 'human stewardship' within God's covenantal relationship with all creation, and humankind within it, to promote a creaturely sense of moral responsibility. This is the hazard of being polemical about contemporary issues. Such reactions tend to generate their own cultural bias, instead of being open-minded to the mystery of the infinite nature of the self-revelatory God.

We may call 'mythology' any human effort to conceive of the divine by human motives and from within human categories. Revelation is contrasted, however, for any revelation of God's own character can come only from God, not from any human suppositions speculating about him within a narrow, prejudicial perspective. As the prophet challenged, 'Who has understood the Spirit of the Lord; or instructed him as his counsellor?' (Isaiah 40:13). This is reiterated by the apostle Paul in 1 Corinthians 2:16. Then Paul adds, 'But we have the mind of Christ.' It is the purpose of this essay to claim that only a Christian interpretation of creation can appropriately transcend any cultural distortions of the nature of the creator. The doctrine of creation therefore requires the doctrine of the incarnation.

Israel's return from Babylonian exile is celebrated in Isaiah 40—55, when 'the Sovereign Lord comes with power, and his arm rules for him' (40:10). The prophet asks, 'To whom, then, will you compare God?' (40:18). To attempt to make any comparison is only to create idols in his place, for as creator God is incomparable. To lift up one's eyes to the starry heavens is to see that God 'created all these' (40:26); 'his understanding no one can fathom' (40:28). Perhaps it was at this period in late antiquity that the belief that God created the world *ex nihilo* first became prominent in Jewish thought. It expresses in shorthand the absolute power of the creator to confront all the human kingdoms that had tyrannized the Jewish people. The Babylonian deliverance was likened to another exodus, like the earlier Egyptian deliverance. This in turn was the recapitulation of creation, so that as God fought and overcame chaos in the creation narrative of Genesis 1, so in the 'chaos' of Egypt, or indeed of Babylon, God has called 'by name' those anonymous slaves, to become his people. As God identifies his creation by setting bounds to each element, so he also protects as well as identifies his people, acting as their creator-redeemer. As the principle of life requires order, so each realm cannot be left void, but is populated by fecundity; this is true of the original creation as it was true of the children of Israel. Everything depends upon God, whether we discern it as creative or redemptive. But when our own creative minds begin to act independently in pride, we begin to mis-construe 'the mind of the Maker', in the words of Dorothy L. Sayers. Perhaps all we can validly think or say of the creator requires a redemptive action on God's part.

The history of the doctrine *creatio ex nihilo* has often had perverted associations with the 'monarchy' of God, however. It has ascribed absolute freedom to God, and in turn assumes that just as 'the divine right of kings' was abused in the 17th century, so God, 'creating from nothing', must be suspected of being a cosmic tyrant today. As the historian Lord Acton said in a letter to Bishop Mandell Creighton in 1887, regarding the discussion on papal infallibility, 'Power corrupts, and absolute power corrupts absolutely.' Deism was certainly a reaction towards such a distorted view of God, making God remote from his creation. When John Milton interpreted the 'Fall of Man', he saw it as a 'happy fall': man had gained his freedom, even if in defiance. At least humankind was now free to rebel against Calvinist distortions of predestination and of sovereign election, as popularly misunderstood, even by John Milton himself. For the deist happily believed that, having created the world, the creator then allowed it to run of its own accord, like a clockmaker might set his invention ticking. By the early 19th century, however, deism was leading to atheism. Napoleon's scientific adviser La Place assured him that there was 'no further need of that hypothesis'—that is, of the existence of the creator.

What this short summary of distorted views of creation illustrates is that we need redeemed minds by which to believe appropriately in the creator and in his creation, and not to assume belief in the spontaneity and autonomy of 'Nature'. For 'the natural' is expressive of our own rebellious, independent spirit, seeking self-regulation rather than divine dependence. As Robert Boyle describes in his late 17th-century monograph, *A Critique of Nature Vulgarly So Called*, 'nature' was a corollary of deism as it was developing culturally in that period of scientific advance.[8]

Now the advance of the 'technological society' has made dependency in human affairs one of the most complex of subjects. We are either afraid of neurotic relationships, speaking of them in terms of co-dependency, or else we are attracted to 'the illusion of omnipotence', that I am free from all restraints in order to pursue self-fulfilment because of all the 'techniques' being invented to help sustain human autonomy. Facing his own death from cancer, Ernest Becker writes, in his insightful book *The Denial of Death*, of the lie we fashion by using other relationships to shore up our own sense of independence, so that a basic human problem lies in overcoming neurotic dependence by divine dependence.[9] It is healthy to recognize in basic humility our inter-dependence since we are not self-regulating mechanisms. At the same time, we need to recognize our freedom to be responsible moral agents, not living in limitless dependence by blaming everyone else for our woes. Endless consumerism is such an addictive dependence, which is profoundly affecting our environment. The need to impress others by accumulating extravagant habits is a misjudged assumption that relationships to 'things' can be a substitute for relationships human or divine, or even a denial that we are relational beings. When environmentalists talk about human disharmony with our environment, therefore, a more basic concern should be our disharmony with our own creatureliness, as God has created us to be. Without knowing and accepting this, we can have a profound delusion about our own nature, our identity, and our place within the cosmic scheme of things. Secular environmental concerns are far too shallow a prognosis of human relations to our environment.

After all his heroic accomplishments, Alexander the Great was rebuked by the philosopher Diogenes, who said to him, 'You are your own worst enemy.' Perhaps, after all the human accomplishments of today, this is still true. One way we may illustrate it is in the simple observation made by the literary critic René Girard, who has explored envy as a basic element of the human condition. Just as we do not have pure or innocent relationships, since they are frequently coloured if not distorted by our narrative of previous relationships, so the individual does not desire spontaneously a direct and immediate relation to the objects of desire. Contrary to this latter view, Girard boldly claims that human desire is mediated, or 'mimetic', as 'desire according to the Other'. This means that we tend to desire 'according to others', in a triangular relationship, not directly in terms of intrinsic preferences. Indeed, Girard goes so far as to suggest that this propensity towards envy is the primary factor behind the emergence of human culture. The key idea is that the human agent suffers from a basic indeterminacy or lack, which self-esteem or self-determination never can fully satisfy. As Girard observes, 'Everybody believes that someone else possesses the self one wants to acquire. That is why everybody experiences desire... Since every desire seeks self-sufficiency, no one really possesses it.'[10]

The advertising industry operates effectively from this basic intuition concerning mimetic desire. Certainly, it dispenses with the myths of human autonomy, rational control, personal lucidity, and of knowing one's place in the scheme of things—environmentally or theologically. For Girard, then, the role of mimetic desire in the human being is the ultimate debunking of the superiority of modern humans, who remain as confused as ever about their role in the created order of things. It also highlights from a very different approach Becker's awareness of the profound illusion of the self-contained individuality of the human being.

Created in the image of God, Girard speaks of our basic character as 'interdividual' rather than 'individual'.[11] This neologism is to emphasize that we are created not as autonomous individuals, but for a relational intent. Yet it is to be neither identical to the Other, nor in slavish subservience to the Other. Of the many things that theologians have observed about the human character of being 'made in the image and likeness of God', relational intent is central. Man placed in creation to have stewardship over it is a reminder of human purpose within the created order. Sexual complement, as male and female, is another expression of human relationality. Deeper still, suggests Sebastian Moore in his book *The Inner Loneliness*, we need to know that we exist for another.[12] I become alive when I engage in love, in compassion, in kindness towards others. Instead of imagining everything 'for oneself', as if everything is 'self-contained', we find that God himself is not self-contained, however self-sufficient the philosopher may judge his attributes of omnipotence, omniscience, omnipresence, and so on. Creation instead manifests the love of God, delighting to be 'for the other', gratuitously and freely creating the world for the well-being of all his creatures. Beyond our understanding lies the reality of God's love. God delights to share, and creation is but the overflow of God's love, expressive of his being, indeed his will and purpose to share his glory with humankind as his companion in creation. As Rowan Williams has expressed succinctly:

*If God's act of creation gratuitously establishes God as the one who is supremely there **for** the world, it seems we must say that God is already one whose being is a 'being for', whose joy is eternally in the joy of another; and since God… does not 'wait upon' becoming an object to another, we are led to think of God's very self as eternal identity in otherness, a self-affirming in giving away.*[13]

If, then, the doctrine of creation is not just about the origin of the world (although that is included), but about the nature of the creator and his relationship to the world, then the mystery of the incarnation must play a central part. This has been motivated in our generation by several approaches: the epistemological, the environmental, the trinitarian and the sabbatical. The exponents of each orientation would admit the importance of the other approaches, while their bias remains towards one orientation. All would agree that the incarnation is the central distinctive of the Christian faith, so each would claim to be essentially a Christian doctrine of creation in the light of the incarnation.

THE EPISTEMOLOGICAL APPROACH TO CREATION AND INCARNATION

Unlike many Christians who are defensive of the doctrine of creation against science, T.F. Torrance (b. 1913) has sought to demonstrate how the rise of empirical Western science has been promoted by Christian theology. By avoiding mechanical and causal explanations within theology, he appeals to the early Fathers, notably Athanasius, as well as to John Calvin later. Following on Karl Barth's theme that only in Christ can a true object of theological study be found, he is hostile to natural theology, for God only can reveal God. But every object must be studied in a manner appropriate to its nature, so there need be no antagonism between the disciplines of theology or of science. This provides harmony and unity of all knowledge in the universe, for God is the source of all things. Torrance is in agreement with Stanley L. Jaki that, beginning in the 13th century, belief in the biblical doctrine of creation created an intellectual climate in the West that provided investigative confidence for the rise of modern science.[14] But Torrance adds to Jaki's suggestion that only when the doctrine of creation was linked with the doctrine of the incarnation, as Calvin did, was there liberation from medieval scholasticism. Then modern science could really advance.[15]

The early Fathers, notably at Nicene (325), struggled over the deity of Christ. The term *homoosion* was used by them to express the consubstantiality of the Father and the Son, in having the same divine nature in two distinct persons. Only, then, through the humanity of Christ is the revelation of the Father made possible, ruling out any alternative ways of seeking to know God; it is an exclusive approach. Using this as an epistemological principle, of knowing according to the intrinsic nature of things as they are, Torrance appreciates that this same principle was applied by modern discoveries of science such as the application of quantum physics in nuclear science.[16] 'Disclosure' is used frequently by Torrance to indicate that the nature of reality is hidden or transcendent, and so requires an intermediate medium through which it may be known. The human knower is then grasped by the disclosure, so that rather than 'holding the truth', one is 'held by the truth'. For reality always transcends the grasp we think we have of it. Faith provides, for Torrance, the guarantee that objectivity is being maintained, so faith is actually seen as a presupposition for knowledge and understanding. The crucial issue is that all knowledge, theological or scientific, must conform to the nature of things as they are in their inherent intelligibility.

If, then, God is love, and in love God created all things, the origin of creation is not explained arbitrarily as *ex nihilo* (which Torrance does not think is a specifically Christian doctrine); but, more biblically, God creates *per Verbum*. The creation was carried out by the Word of God, eternally *homoousion* with the Father, and yet who became incarnate, assuming human form in space and time. So Torrance would argue that creation alone is insufficient for an ontology of the universe, since it can only be understood by the further doctrine of the incarnation, of the Word who became incarnate in human form. This is following the argument of Athanasius, who believed that there can be no proper understanding of creation without the incarnate Word of God.[17] Torrance goes further in positing that the empirical development of modern science would also not have been possible without the incarnation. Here is where scientists, Christian as well as non-Christian, debate with Torrance, a debate well developed by Tapio Luoma in his recent book *Incarnation and Physics*.[18]

Having opened the way to Torrance's way of knowing appropriately, much could be explored about his distinction between myth and reality. He interprets the mythical as expressive of human subjective distortions of the truth, whereas reality discloses its own intrinsic character. Our cultural perceptions of the creator all tend to be expressive of the mythological, but 'reality' itself is an evasive concept, as other critics of Torrance's thought have been quick to point out. For Torrance remains vulnerable when realism is conceived too narrowly within philosophical conceptions, even when he seeks to maintain that the incarnation is basic to understanding reality. Actually he infers from the two Christian doctrines of accommodation and of election, how God permits us to know reality. First, God permits us to know his being by condescending to the same creaturely level as ours. In Jesus Christ, God has shown us how we can be truly creaturely and learn to know God appropriately as our creator. Second, 'divine election' means that the initiative of knowing God comes from God's love, not from our initiative. As the apostle John expressed it, 'We love because he first loved us' (1 John 4:19). God's election excludes all human initiatives, making us aware that the preceding intelligibility of the universe was already there, given by God, and not achieved exclusively by human intelligence. As the astronomer Kepler put it, the human task is simply 'to think God's thoughts after him'.

This, then, is how the element of 'compulsion' to think appropriately is argued by Torrance. He sums up his definition of election as follows:

Election refers to the eternal decision which is nothing less than the Love of God himself is, in action; it is the unconditional self-giving of God in the undeflecting constancy of his Grace, which... flows freely and equally to all irrespective of any claim or worth or reaction on their part.[19]

He then concludes:

The Incarnation, therefore, may be regarded as the eternal decision or election of God in his Love not to be confined, as it were, within himself alone, but to pour himself out in unrestrained Love upon the world which he himself has made and to actualize that Love in Jesus Christ in such a way within the condition of our spatio-temporal existence that he constitutes the one Mediator between God and man through whom we may all freely participate in the unconditional Love and Grace of God.[20]

The incarnation transformed our created status, first because Christ alone is now seen to be the image and likeness of God, and so our true humanity is alone in him. Second, as long as we remain outside of Christ, we shall always remain in disharmony with his divine purpose for the well-being of all creation.

THE ENVIRONMENTAL APPROACH OF JURGEN MOLTMANN

Perhaps it was the impact of living in the nuclear age that most impressed Torrance to think out the consequences of a unified field theory such as Einstein's $E=MC^2$. Our next theologian, Jurgen Moltmann, lived through the consequences of Fascism in Germany and, more recently, has become alerted to other cultural challenges, not least of which is the ecological crisis. This began to surface in the early 1960s, and it has challenged Moltmann to examine the creator's relationship with his creation, as well as the kind of human relationship with creation that has precipitated the ecological crisis. Exploitative domination has taken place as the consequence of analytical, objectifying thinking, which views the creation pragmatically in a context of objects, detached from the observer, and evaluated from a utilitarian perspective. Rather, an ecological theology is needed that is a participatory kind of knowledge, restoring the sense of community with nature, respecting its independence and participating in mutual relationships with it.

Moltmann touches upon this in his book *God in Creation*.[21] Human beings have a distinctive place in nature, but not an exclusive, dominating place, he argues. The praxis of specific ecological recommendations for this agenda is disappointing in its lack of specific and concrete proposals, however. It is the familiar game professionals play of 'passing the buck', so that theologians are not ecologists, as ecologists are not theologians. Perhaps this is what a Christian should be—a synthesizer and practitioner at the same time; not just a specialist!

The strength of Moltmann's theology is his central principle of relatedness. He understands things not in themselves, but as they relate to other things. As he observes, 'In reality relationships are just as primal as the things themselves.'[22] Open Systems theory or symbiosis claim scientific support for this principle in nature, but he grounds it on the character of the triune God in *perichoresis*. God is not a divine hierarchy, but one of mutual indwelling as a perichoretic community of Father, Son and Holy Spirit. Likewise, God's relationship with his creation is one of mutual indwelling. God's openness to the world is such that the relationships of the three persons do not form an inclusive circle in the heavens, but an open community in which the life of all creation can participate. For a prisoner of war in World War II, as Moltmann was, this is a great alternative!

But Moltmann goes further, in affirming that God has a trinitarian history with creation, in which God not only acts on the world but is affected by the world. He accepts that such contingency must mean that the trinitarian relationships themselves change as human history is taken within them, yet this trinitarian history has the kingdom of God as its goal. This means that God will be all in all—a form of panentheism, in which God will be glorified in his indwelling of creation as creation will be glorified in its participation of God. This is going much further than Jesus' prayer of John 17, in which *perichoresis* is defined personally as between the Lord and the believers, not within all creation itself.

The axis of Moltmann's theological position is, then, that God is transcendent beyond the world, as it dwells in him; and yet, because he is immanent within it, he dwells in it. The universe, he argues, is not a closed system, but 'a system that is open—open for God and for his future'.[23] As a result, Moltmann is very open to including scientific theories of evolution within his theology. He sees a broad interpretation of the whole history of nature as an evolutionary process, so first of all he has to overcome hermeneutical objection to the view of creation as having an initial beginning at the fiat of God's will. Rather, such 'openness' posits creation as 'unfinished', positively welcoming the scientific understanding of evolutionary change. Second, Moltmann would seek redress from the transcendent view of God over creation by more bias towards the mutuality of relationships, seeking more focus upon the immanent creative Spirit at work in the processes of evolution, so he maintains that the creative activity of the immanent Spirit is not distinguishable from the processes of nature. He is trying to see 'nature' and 'creation' as one category, not as a scientific and a theological series of distinctions. Third, he accepts the evolutionary history of the human being as entirely appropriate to his understanding of human creation, but what he desires is to see every product of evolution as having its own meaning before God.

So how does Moltmann's evolutionary consciousness differ from Teilhard de Chardin's thoroughgoing evolutionary process of salvation history? Moltmann responds that the evolutionary process may be creative but it is not redemptive. In *The Way of Jesus Christ*, he states:

Teilhard does seem to have overlooked the ambiguity of evolution itself, and therefore to have paid no attention to evolution's victims. Evolution always means natural selection. Many living things are sacrificed in order that 'the fittest'—which means the most effective and adaptable—may survive... in the same process milliards of living things fall by the wayside and disappear into evolution's rubbish bin.[24]

Then he adds, 'The various processes of evolution in nature and humanity can only be brought into a positive relationship to Christ, the perfecter of creation, if Christ is perceived as a victim among other victims.'[25] In other words, if evolution cannot be confused with redemption, then neither should teleology be confused with eschatology. For whereas evolutionary teleology appears random and leaves its many victims behind in its un-disclosed goal, eschatology is the perfecting of all created things in the eternal purpose of God's glory. Moltmann, then, has not overcome the tension between 'nature' and 'creation', or 'evolution' and God's 'redemptive purpose'.[26] In fact, his concept of the 'openness of God' opens up too much to speculation that is not adequately grounded in the Bible.

TRINITARIAN CREATION IN THE INTERPRETATION OF COLIN GUNTON

The cultural concern in which Colin Gunton (1941–2003) was engaged, to communicate the doctrine of creation, is the broader concern of modernity and especially of late modernity. He answered some of these issues, such as the problems of reality or of the particular, of relatedness, and of the rootless will, in his Bampton lectures, *The One, the Three, and the Many*. Unlike Moltmann, who does not take the Church Fathers seriously enough, Gunton traced the importance of Ireneaus for a trinitarian understanding of God, as Torrance accepted Athanasius. Gunton argued that part of the responsibility for the modern fragmentation of culture, and especially its loss of a coherent sense of meaning and truth, is to be laid at the door of Christian theology's traditional tendency to a monolithic conception of God and of truth, rather than recognizing the intrinsic relational character of God as Trinity. Instead, he presented the view that God relates himself to the world in a variety of ways, in wisdom, by speech, in Christ, by his Spirit. The loss of this relatedness leads to the modern plight of 'disengagement' and of 'instrumentality' in our attitudes to reality,[27] so it was in concern for the relational recovery of truth and reality that Gunton wanted to explore a trinitarian understanding of creation.

The failure of the Enlightenment project to establish truth by reason alone is only one of the consequences of the rejection of God in the contemporary world. Rather, Gunton traced back to what he would also dismiss as the Platonic dualism of theologians such as Augustine for theological causes of the vulnerability of Western theology to its rejection by the modern culture.[28] He sought to explore relatedness, not so much for understanding creatureliness as for 'rethinking createdness'. By this he meant that the foundations of reality are either viewed as the particularity of the one, or else as the universal claim, neither of which are effectively united. For all knowledge derives from some kind of faith, whether it be in the intelligibility of the universe or in the benevolence of God. To seek foundations in rationality alone is 'a will-of-the-wisp'.

It was in the doctrine of the Trinity that Gunton sought an integration of the particular and the universal. As he quotes from Gregory of Nazianzus, 'No sooner do I conceive of the One than I am illumined by the splendour of the Three: no sooner do I distinguish them than I am carried back to the One.'[29] That is, he recognized the dynamic dialectic between the oneness and the threeness of God as being of such a kind that the two are given equal weight in the processes of thought. The application of this is not for environmental concerns such as Moltmann expresses, but more broadly how the individual and society can cohere instead of becoming antithetical; or again how eternity and infinity can be viewed not as oppressive, but in harmony with space and time, so that the culture need not embrace only the contemporary.

Gunton also appealed to *perichoresis*, so that the particularity of each person of the Trinity is not one without the other.[30] He too desired a theology of relatedness, of 'shared being', so that we in turn do not need to opt for individualism or community, but find we are constituted by 'shared being'. Just as the triune God has communion-in-otherness, so too human creation has its true being in relationship. Humankind is of a social kind, 'male and female he created them' (Genesis 1:27), so that the world is interpreted appropriately because we bear the image of God socially, not individualistically. Gunton admitted that this ideal was forfeited at the fall, so that such communion depends upon atonement, but his approach remains implicit of the incarnation, not explicit as the two previous theological approaches have spelt out. As he argued, if there is to be any talk of the incarnation, it must presuppose the existence of the triune God, for it holds that the one through whom the world was made has become part of that world in order to redeem it from its bondage to decay. Indeed, 'when we are able to see what God achieves through the Son and the Spirit… we are better able to develop an eschatology which is concerned with the completion of that which was established in the beginning'.[31] The purpose of the incarnation is to direct creation towards the achievement of its true destiny.

A SABBATICAL APPROACH TO CREATION

All these and other theologians do recognize strongly that there is an eschatological purpose in creation. This may be summed up in the theme of the Sabbath of creation, which distinguishes it from nature, for the universe is created by the Word of God, then blessed and sanctified. Often it has been assumed that the crown of creation is humanity, in which God pronounced not only that it was 'good', but 'very good' (Genesis 1:31). However, God rests only on the seventh day, when all creation has been accomplished. Then it becomes possible for humanity to rest in it also. For the restlessness of the human spirit in rebellion, independence, and mis-use of creation are the marks of the fall, in not letting God's creation 'to be' as God wills it be, but to be misconceived and misused by the distortion of the human spirit. Could it be, then, that 'the keeping of the Sabbath' is an ethical injunction for us to be true stewards of ourselves, as well as of the created world?

In the summary text of Genesis 2:2–3, the seventh day is marked three times, indicating its significance above every other day. Indeed, it takes on a biblical significance for perfection or completion in the rest of scripture. As Bruce Walkte has noted, 'In the first days space is subdued; on the seventh time is sanctified. This day is blessed to refresh the earth.'[32] As Hebrews 4:3–11 reminds us, it is eschatological in orientation, looking forward to the eternal, redemptive Sabbath rest. A seven-day week was unique to Israel, and its blessing and sanctity marked off God's dealings with his people from all other nations. In other cultures, the seventh day might be a cosmic, cataclysmic event, to be feared, and certainly no celebration of rest. Other peoples in the ancient Near East built temples to celebrate the cosmologies of their creator gods, as a sign of their conquest of the wild forces of chaos, but Yahweh chose a temporal shrine in which the Israelites could celebrate weekly rest from their labours.

Not even the seasons of the year interfered with the weekly rhythm of Sabbath rest, although they were celebrated in the three feasts of the lambing season (the Passover), the grain harvest (Pentecost) and the grape harvest (the feast of Tabernacles). Thus, by the observation of the Sabbath, Israel confessed weekly that their Lord was Lord of all. In turn, Sabbath-keeping was a sign that the creator had set Israel apart for a special covenant relationship with him (Exodus 31:17). Indeed, it reminded Israel that they had been slaves in Egypt, but had been set free from oppressive servitude to rest in his redemption (Deuteronomy 5:15). Now in the incarnate Christ, argues the apostle, the redeemed have their 'sabbath rest' in Christ, not in mere legal observance of the rabbinical code of conduct (Colossians 2:16–17). For it is now, in the preaching of the gospel of Christ, that the Sabbath rest has been fulfilled, so that we rest fully in Christ (Hebrews 4:1–11).

But the technical control of time, time by the clock (*chronos*), has become a new mode of reality, which puts humanity at the centre of the universe and which eclipses the relational reality of leaving our times in the hands of our creator.[33] In his meditations on the Sabbath, A.J. Heschel argues that technology has sought to overcome space at the cost of time: 'In technical civilization we expend time to gain space... but time is the heart of existence... But the higher goal of spiritual living is not to amass information, but to face sacred moments'—yes, moments of insight that may have eternal significance.[34] Instead, 'the day of the Lord'—eventful time (*kairos*)—has been replaced by the jejune, empty modern incantation of 'the future', that is becoming ever more vacuous.

Although the order of creation stands behind the Sabbath, yet, says Jesus, the Sabbath is meant for humanity (Mark 2:27). Indeed, its central significance was, and still lies, in the sanctification of God's people. Much theological concern with distinguishing 'creation' from 'nature', or indeed the meaning of 'creatureliness' or of 'createdness', misses the ethical issue that it is only as a sanctified people that Christians can appreciate the contrast between nature and creation, not just as scientists or theologians. By keeping the Sabbath day, argues John Calvin, we come to recognize Christ more 'in our living experience, than in vain and high-flown speculation'.[35] The symbol of the Sabbath reminds God's people that 'the one who began a good work among you will bring it to completion by the day of Jesus Christ' (Philippians 1:6, NRSV). The Sabbath reflects on faith in the creator-redeemer, who is Alpha and Omega, the beginning and the end. As he consummates his work of creation, so he will complete his purposes in redemption as the incarnate Lord. It is a means of saving knowledge, and a gift given us by God's grace in Christ, through his Holy Spirit.

The mystery of the Sabbath is disclosed in the incarnate Christ. For as Calvin understood so clearly, Christ is the true Man, humanity as the creator intended him to be, and yet he is also our divine mediator, in whom and through whom God has done everything—not for himself but for the sake of all creation, including humanity. Therefore, on the Sabbath day, the Christian believer can put away his or her anxieties and repose in the triune God. For as Jesus returned to his home town of Nazareth, he entered the synagogue on the Sabbath day to declare, 'Today this scripture is fulfilled in your hearing' (Luke 4:21). No longer does it remain a legalistic remnant of Judaism, but it is given its full meaning in the finished work of Christ. It continues to challenge human arrogance, independence of spirit, and the technical-mindedness that confuses means with ends, so that efficiency becomes a goal in itself. The crisis of many Christian institutions today is just this: when original vision is supplanted by growth in technical skills, personal vision is eventually destroyed. Just as rabbinical legalism lost sight of the original creation mandate, and Calvinistic legalism over 'Sunday' destroyed 'Sabbath keeping', so now technical skills threaten to destroy all credibility for our creaturely mandate of 'Christian ministry'.

For at the heart of the Pharisees' controversy with Jesus over Sabbath-keeping is a misconception of piety. It makes an idol of piety, or indeed of celibacy, or of 'ministry', instead of each pointing iconically to our relationship with the triune God. Christ proclaims that 'the Son of Man is Lord even of the Sabbath' (Matthew 12:8; Mark 2:28; Luke 6:5), but the ability to do certain things, whether it be 'keeping the Sabbath', or 'being celibate', or 'doing ministry', remain the work of the Holy Spirit, who gives us the freedom—not the bondage—to do them. For the purpose and proper use of Sabbath-keeping is to enjoy true worship and be freed from all worldly cares for that purpose. It has a healing ministry within our lives, as Jesus himself healed on the Sabbath day. Also it anticipates eschatologically the healing of all creation. It restores freedom to every creature that now 'groans in travail' (Romans 8:22, RSV), a mystery not yet fully manifest nor understood by us.

Thus, in an age of self-identifying, perhaps creation itself cannot be celebrated adequately without human beings accepting our true 'sabbatical identity'. It is our joyful and worshipful repose in God the Father, through the Holy Spirit, in the work of Christ. Rest on the Sabbath signifies the goodness of God's creation, as well as of our salvation in the incarnate Christ. This is well summarized in Calvin's reflections on Hebrews 4:10:

For here we must always begin, when we speak of a godly and holy life, that man being in a manner dead to himself, should allow God to live in him, that he should abstain from his own works, so as to give place to God to work. We must indeed confess, that then only is our life rightly formed when it becomes subject to God. But through inbred corruption that is never the case, until we rest from our own works; nay, such is the opposition between God's government and our corrupt affections, that he cannot work in us until we rest. But though the completion of this rest cannot be attained in this life, yet we ought ever to strive for it.[36]

⁘

REDEEMING CREATION IN
THE SHADOW OF WAR

Chris Naylor, A Rocha Lebanon

Early in the morning the Aammiq marsh lies in the shadow of Mount Hermon, the dominant peak in the eastern mountain chain that defines the Bekaa Valley in Lebanon. In recent years, other shadows have passed over the wetland as the course of war has ebbed and flowed across the green hillsides and fertile plains in which the marsh is situated. If you visit the marsh today, you will see crumbling tank emplacements that face each other just metres from either side of the open water, showing how the marshland provided a strategic frontline for opposing forces.

When the A Rocha Lebanon project first began, the shadow of war had only recently left, but the consequences were self-evident. For example, 700,000 trees had been cut down in the area, hillside forests were opened up to the ravages of goats after the armies had opened roads into the mountains to connect their forces, and areas of land were strewn with landmines, making them dangerous to enter. Perhaps the deepest wounds were found in the hardening of people's attitudes towards one another. Community was set against community, corruption had grown and the struggle for survival in the aftermath of war had led to exploitation of both the land and local men and women.

The wetlands suffered from the years under the shadow of war and exploitation. Now the land is sick. It has been blasted indiscriminately by hunters, scorched by uncontrolled fires, and has become the waste bin of West Bekaa. Into this context, A Rocha Lebanon was birthed. Our earliest efforts were focused on reversing the years of habitat loss. This involved a comprehensive mapping of the marsh area. We set out boundary markers to limit the land used for agriculture. Our scientific studies were aimed at putting Aammiq back on the conservation map. Bird, butterfly, mammal and plant surveys showed that, despite the damage, the wetland was still

98

an oasis for wildlife, albeit on the brink of disaster. The access for four-wheel-drive vehicles and hunters was closed and a public awareness and environmental education programme was put into operation, directed at schoolchildren, university and college students and the local village communities. Now former hunting grounds are places where children can go 'pond dipping', students can go bird-watching and women's groups seeking inspiration for craft activities are able to use the wonders of the marshland for their creative work.

Our restoration operation needed to work on several different levels. First and foremost, we had to restore the natural habitats. Marginal fields were returned to flooded pastures and reed beds, water was redirected to lengthen the period of flooding, and hunting was controlled. Equally important, relationships needed to be restored and reconciliation brought about between different communities and their relationships with the land. In the end, farming contracts became more transparent and agreements were reached between shepherds and landowners. Above all, people gained a renewed respect for the wetland and its wildlife, and the communities began to heal the wounds of the past. All the reconciliation between the land and the people has brought the Aammiq marsh out of the shadow of war.

JESUS AND THE RESURRECTION

Sarah Tillett

The events of Boxing Day 2004 meant that 2005 began with appalling scenes of devastation splashed across our television screens and newspapers. We watched horrified as the scale of the disaster across the Indian Ocean unfurled before our eyes. Hundreds of thousands of human lives and livelihoods were lost to the sea. Complete communities were destroyed, vegetation swamped and uprooted, and soil washed away.

The horror of the disaster brought to mind Old Testament imagery and prompted the inevitable question of belief in a God who would either be the cause of or allow such human misery. A significant factor that influenced the scale of devastation was poverty. Poverty broke into the living-rooms of Western households in a daily onslaught never before experienced; it brought the shocking reality of the economic injustices of our world into the spotlight. If there had been better infrastructure, communications and sophisticated earthquake warning systems, perhaps the story would have been different.

Certainly, scientific technology makes an invaluable contribution towards the quality of life on earth, but on its own, is it enough? The human condition is such that we need more than scientific intervention; we need a change of heart. If our response to the human and environmental devastation of our world is shaped by our knowledge and understanding of God, then, as this book argues, we have a wisdom and a hope that transcends the merely physical and human.

God is most clearly known through the life, death and resurrection of his son Jesus Christ. In fact, in Jesus' resurrection we meet with Christ's victory over sin and death and are invited to be part of and witnesses to a new, redeemed, transformed life for the whole of God's creation.

Whichever way we look at this truth, it demands a response from us. We cannot remain passive.

The problem is that absolute belief in the resurrection has been a stumbling block for many people throughout the history of Christianity. Yet, all the biblical truths of God's continued providence hang from the great mystery of the resurrection. Western culture particularly has been influenced by early Greek neo-Platonic influences, which tended to deny the goodness of the material and physical world, including the goodness of the human body, and reduced Christ's resurrection to a merely spiritual resurrection. In addition, the Enlightenment philosophy of Descartes introduced the idea of the autonomous knower: 'I think, therefore I am'.[1] This assumes that we can know without the exercise of belief, an argument that has in recent years been challenged.

The creation of the autonomous mind dismissed all sense of mystery, of the spiritual realm, of divinity other than its own god-like powers. It was a rejection of the presence of God in human life and the witness of that presence through the ages. It's not hard to see how damaging this was to the transcendent mysteries revealed in the scriptures (such as the resurrection) and the consequent changes in the development of theological knowledge. Reality was reduced to the merely descriptive and speculative, and dismissed as subjective the kind of participatory knowledge in which the observer was personally involved. If the act of faith is real, it is always something that demands from us more than our own understanding can fathom. It does not contradict, but goes beyond that understanding. If Christ is not risen, our faith is in vain.

The beginning and end of any question to do with knowing Jesus must lie in enriching our understanding of the resurrection, because the resurrection is the experience at the centre of the Christian faith, from which point we come to understand the doctrines of the incarnation and the Trinity. Roman Catholic theologian James Alison reminds us that the Christian faith, the norm of the Church, derives from received witness, the witness of the apostles to Jesus' life and ministry, death and resurrection. Without the resurrection, all we would have would be just another dead body. He says:

The apostles witness to the irruption of a happening into their lives and one that could be experienced in a variety of ways. It was not simply a fact that they could then tack on to the end of the creed, so that it would be a fuller account of what *had happened. It was what made it possible for there to be a creed at all. If there had been no resurrection, there would have been no New Testament, since the New Testament **is** the witness of the apostles to the resurrection, including their new found ability to understand what led to it. Without it there would have been no new story to tell.*[2]

The Gospels are not biographies of Jesus; they are witnesses to the experience of the resurrection and the rewriting of the apostles' experiences of their relationship with Jesus in the light of the resurrection.[3] Their witness is not just a witness *to* the fact of the resurrection as an event, as one would witness a road accident; it is a witness *from* the perspective of the resurrection. This unprecedented event caused the disciples radically to change their understanding of who God is, and, just as importantly, brought about a new understanding of what it is to be human, which began to transform their lives.

It changed humble fishermen into international heroes and martyrs, and it caused them to rethink the whole of their lives, their relationship with their culture and its values, and, as we understand from the apostle Paul, their relationship to all of creation (Colossians 1:15–23). In a similar way today, we transmit the truth of the resurrection to one another. We don't believe in the resurrection on our own; we believe it as we receive its transforming nature through relationships with others and through the Holy Spirit.

Christians over the centuries have meditated on the resurrection accounts of the Gospel writers as a way of getting under the skin of the first-hand experiences. Luke's tale of the two little-known disciples on the road to Emmaus helps us to understand the impact of the risen Christ on the disciples (Luke 24:13–35). As we imagine ourselves walking with the disciples and try to understand how they might have been feeling, their experience resonates with us and expands our own relationship with the risen Christ as we grow to understand how the truths of Christianity keep us full of hope in the face of so much that is wrong with the world, with the Church, and with ourselves.

When Jesus died on Good Friday, the disciples' relationship with him ended in tragedy. All of the emotions they had invested in Jesus were now left in a vacuum, worsened by the guilt they felt at having abandoned Jesus. As James Alison says:

Their relationship with Jesus was for ever and abruptly severed. They had no hope of waiting to see if Jesus would come back from the Crimea. Death was not like the Crimea. There were no signs that something might change, that God might revoke death. There was just termination; they were left like live cables off which a computer had been yanked and burned, leaving them powerless to receive or transmit information.[4]

No doubt their sense of desolation was compounded by the atmosphere of fear that would have surrounded them, and their awareness of the dangerous situation they were in because of their association with Jesus.

As Jesus joined the two travellers on the road, he listened to their discouragement and then initiated conversation by asking them what they were discussing. Surprised by his lack of awareness of the recent events, they told him everything. We can sense the despair that these disciples felt. They had regarded Jesus as more than a prophet. He had been the one who would overthrow the oppressive Roman occupation, the one chosen by God to redeem Israel from pagan domination once and for all. There was nothing in the Jewish resurrection hope, spoken of through the Old Testament prophets, to prepare them for Jesus' crucifixion or his resurrection. They had no framework of reference to interpret the events that had taken place. Nevertheless, in the midst of their despair they were about to experience a radical reinterpretation of the scriptures (Luke 24:25–27).

Like everyone in Israel at that time, they had been reading the scriptures through the wrong lenses. On the road, Jesus revealed that the story of God's redemption of Israel was not from suffering but through suffering. The suffering of the world would be taken on by the Messiah. Jesus went through the whole story from Genesis to Chronicles,[5] showing that in order to bring in God's new creation he had to suffer and die and rise again (v. 27).

The next initiative was taken by the disciples. As they approached the village, it became apparent that Jesus was travelling on, and they decided to invite this stranger who had accompanied them on their way to stay and eat with them (v. 29). They had no idea of the significance of their invitation as Jesus sat down with them. It reminds us that small decisions can have very important consequences. In the context of the openness of their invitation, they become more human; it is the awakening of their understanding that God just might be doing something beyond their present circumstances and revealing a truth beyond that known through the old covenant. The veil that had once protected Moses from the glory of God is being lifted (2 Corinthians 3:14–18).

Up until this moment, Jesus' identity has been a mystery; the two disciples have no idea who he is. One important aspect of the resurrection is that Jesus' identity is revealed to the disciples by the evidence of his death. It is the presence of the marks of his death that prove to the disciples that he is the same man. John's Gospel insists that the risen Jesus had the marks of the nails in his hands and feet (John 20:24–31), while Luke's Gospel suggests as much when Jesus stops to eat with his companions (24:30). The key to the explanation that he gives the disciples of the true meaning of the scriptures—that the Messiah must suffer and die before entering into his glory—is realized in the shared meal that followed. Jesus' presence and the revelation of the meaning of his death are part of the same experience for the disciples (v. 32). He did not only appear as the risen Lord, but he appeared as the crucified-and-risen Lord.

There is more to the mystery of the resurrection than the physical appearance of the risen Jesus to his disciples; far more difficult to understand is the significance of its effect on the disciples. But if we try to understand the actual experiences as he appears to his followers, experiences that are hinted at in the New Testament accounts, but which are hard for us to identify because we read them with the benefit of foreknowledge (we know what is coming next), we discover the power of God's love in a vital and transforming way.

Alison categorizes the experience of the resurrection in three ways—as gratuity, forgiveness and mission. It was gratuitous because for Jesus it was an act of love by the Father, and for the disciples it was a giving back of a freely loving person. It was experienced as forgiveness because Jesus appeared to the disciples without reproach, and by his presence they experienced the grace of forgiveness (they no longer felt remorse or guilt for abandoning him). Jesus tells the disciples in Luke 24:47 that repentance and forgiveness of sins are to be preached in his name to all nations, and in John 20:22–23 he says, 'Receive the Holy Spirit. If you forgive the sins of any, they are forgiven them; if you retain the sins of any, they are retained' (NRSV). The resurrection was experienced as mission, because the grace and forgiveness that came through the risen Christ's presence were given to the disciples so as to be given away by them to others. As Alison sums it up, 'The utterly other, gratuitously present as forgiveness, doesn't just irrupt into the lives of the disciples; it sends them to the ends of the earth.'[6]

Resurrection is an extraordinary affirmation by God of the material world, because God shows his love through the physical presence of Christ's slaughtered but resurrected body. The resurrection life includes the human death of Jesus. It is not just an affirmation of humanity through Jesus, but an affirmation of the material created world. Jesus took his place with his Father and raised frail human nature to glory. In order to put an end to the domination of death, Christ, through God, has to be greater than nature. Accordingly, the resurrection involves an act of re-creation, a correction to the whole created order. It is the transfiguration of the world of death and nature, of life and death. It is the abolition, within nature, of death, corruption and decay.

Jesus shared many meals with his followers, and the meal he shared with the two disciples at Emmaus points forward to the time when sharing and breaking bread and wine became the central symbolic action of the Christian faith. Although Jesus was no longer physically present, the people of God would discover him living with and in them through the sharing of this meal. The road to Emmaus is the beginning of Jesus' invitation to each one of us to be led out of the slavery of sin and rebellion against God and to accompany him on the journey to the promised land.

The promised land is not some faraway distant place. Tom Wright, in his book *The Resurrection of the Son of God*, confirms that it is the real world, which the real God made and still grieves over. It is the real world in which the resurrection took place and was witnessed by the disciples, 'not as a bizarre miracle, but as the beginning of the new creation'.[7] The creator grieved so much over what had gone wrong, over humanity's rebellion and the dust and decay of his world, that he planned from the beginning the way in which he would redeem and rescue it. Jesus ushered in the kingdom of God's reign here on earth and offered a way for us, God's image bearers, to assist in restoring the whole of creation.

In Paul's letter to the church in Rome, he explains that the Spirit of God is at work doing what the law could not achieve (Romans 8:3): giving new life, resurrection life (v. 11). The promise of resurrection is that we shall be rescued from corruption and decay and death. God promised the coming Messiah in Psalm 2:8, 'Ask of me, and I will make the nations your heritage, and the ends of the earth your possession' (NRSV). This was the promise to Abraham and his ancestors (inheritance of the promised land: Exodus 15:17) and it is the same promise for all who follow God today.

In Romans, Paul declares that the whole of creation is waiting (groaning) for us to partner with God in redeeming that which has been subjected to the fall (8:22). Paul gives us a panoramic view of the whole of God's plan of salvation for all he has created. All the present suffering in the world will pale into insignificance compared to 'the glory about to be revealed to us' (v. 18). We will be sharing in the Messiah's inheritance and therefore in his redeeming rule over the whole world. It is what all creation is waiting for, because that is the time for it to be rescued from decay and death.

As we saw so powerfully in the Indian Ocean at the beginning of 2005, those who live in the vulnerable places of the world—beside an earth-quake fault-line, or in the volcanic regions of the world—can encounter creation as a mass of destructive energy. But God's covenant faithfulness, declared through his promises to Abraham, Noah and Moses, reveal that one day all of the fallenness and brokenness of the world will be put right. Creation fell into disrepair through human rebellion, but now God's plan for its restoration is revealed. This plan involves God's people taking their place in obedience to him, worshipping him and taking good care of all that he has created. When the people of God are glorified (Romans 8:18), then the whole of creation will be made new.

This resurrection perspective has huge implications for the way we regard our responsibility towards the earth and everything in it, and for the way we think about the future of the world. There is a tension between the 'now' and the 'not yet' fulfilled. Our hope comes from the certainty we have in God's final restoration of all that he has made.

Since Pentecost, God's Spirit has been at work, renewing his people. We are not set apart from the suffering of the world, just as God did not avoid suffering. Instead he came to dwell in the midst of suffering through his Son, and now lives among us through the presence and power of his Spirit. Our answer to the degradation, pain and suffering of the fallen creation is to be caught up in all that God is doing through his Spirit, to share the pain of the world and to respond actively to the needs of the world.

Wendell Berry is a Kentucky farmer, author, poet and essayist who, in one of his most radical poems, reaches into the core of the resurrection mystery. In 'Manifesto: The Mad Farmer Liberation Front', he confronts full-on the selfish materialism of Western society:

> Love the Quick Profit, the annual raise,
> Vacation without pay. Want more
> Of everything ready-made. Be afraid
> To know your neighbours and to die.
> And you will have a window in your head.
> Not even your future will be a mystery anymore.
> … When they want you to buy something
> They will call you. When they want you
> to die for profit they will let you know.

He goes on to summons people to a more radical, countercultural way of life:

> So, friends, every day do something
> that won't compute. Love the Lord.
> Love the World. Work for nothing.
> Take all that you have and be poor.
> Love someone who does not deserve it…

Berry's work has been motivated by the desire to make himself at home in this world and in his native chosen place.

'Manifesto' ends with these lines:

> Be like the Fox who makes more tracks than necessary,
> some in the wrong direction.
> Practice resurrection.[8]

✤

BEE ORCHID ON THE MINET SITE

Dave Bookless, A Rocha UK

In 2004 a good friend of mine died, in his 50s, after a long struggle with cancer. He was an ecologist, and he was a Christian. Graham was also deeply involved with A Rocha, both in the UK and through volunteering in Lebanon.

When, during 1998, as a local vicar and amateur wildlife enthusiast, I first had the crazy idea that more than 70 acres of derelict London wasteland could become the Minet Country Park, Graham was the first experienced naturalist to walk around the site with me. It was a very slow walk. Every few steps, Graham would stop and pick up an insect or point at a plant. He talked about the food-plant an insect needed, the predators it faced, the plants it pollinated. He spoke with immense knowledge, but also with child-like wonder at the detail, the diversity, the interdependence within the natural world. Afterwards I reflected that it was just a little like walking with God in the garden of Eden—a God who saw all that he had made as 'very good'.

Graham went on to help A Rocha UK in many practical ways, cycling across London to attend prayer meetings, advising us on many ecological, educational and planning matters. His passion for God and his passion for creation were inseparable. When he knew that he had inoperable cancer, he faced it quietly and without fear. Perhaps his closeness to the natural world helped him to accept the place of death in the cycle of life, more than many in our death-denying culture. Certainly his Christian faith gave him assurance that the one who has reconciled all things to himself through Jesus would take his worn-out body and remake it.

Graham's funeral was as remarkable as his life. It was attended by colleagues from the London Ecology Unit and elsewhere, as well as by many friends, family and church members. He chose every detail of the service, from the cardboard coffin decorated with native wildflowers to the hymns (including 'O Lord my God, when I in awesome wonder consider all the works thy hand has made…' climaxing in 'When Christ shall come with shout of acclamation and take me home, what joy shall fill my heart'). The service was full of Bible passages, focusing on Jesus, the one for whom all things were made, and in whom all things find their home. Graham was going home to prepare for the renewal of all things in Christ.

Back on the Minet site, we had also experienced a kind of resurrection. Layers of rubbish and rubble were removed. Some areas were landscaped and replanted; others were cleared, allowing native plants to regenerate. One older Christian, walking around the site, talked of how, after 40 years, this had given her a completely new understanding of redemption. At the weekend we celebrated the newly opened Minet Country Park, we found a single bee orchid growing in an area of disturbed ground. Its spores must have lain dormant for years before it pushed through the soil to give us such joy. The bee orchid spoke of resurrection from death and decay, of the tomb-like ground breaking open in the springtime of new life. As with the seamlessness of Graham's life, death and resurrection, it was a reminder of the sure hope contained in Christ, the firstfruits of the new creation.

COMMUNITY AND OUR INHERITANCE

Miranda Harris

'Belonging is a terrible but beautiful reality,' wrote Jean Vanier. 'We do not discover who we are, we do not reach true humanness in a solitary state, we discover it through mutual dependency, in weakness, in learning through belonging.'[1] This is made very difficult for us in a culture that places great emphasis on self-sufficiency and independence, actively discouraging the model of personal and economic interdependence that we find in the Bible. We are used to privatizing our experience of life, and then placing ownership upon it: my family; my job, my money, my faith. Nowhere is this tendency more dangerous than in the community of believers, where it isolates people from one another and effectively denies the gospel its power to transform relationships and become visible in a world badly in need of some good news.

In the ecstasy and ignorance of my own conversion experience, and with the sublime confidence of one setting out into an entirely black-and-white world, I assumed that my wordy proclamations to friends and family (and sometimes people on trains) were introducing God for the very first time— a completely fresh set of footprints, as it were. I was to learn a lot about God's presence and my own pride in the experience of helping to run the first A Rocha Centre for ten years, and began to detect his footprints and fingerprints everywhere: a whiff of the fragrance of Jesus lurking around someone who has not given his life to Christ; a tender heart showing evident forgiveness while clearly not yet having received forgiveness from the Lord herself. Increasingly I became aware of a secret history unfolding in every life in which God, acknowledged or not, is the protagonist. Sometimes the very people protesting the loudest spend the most time thinking about him. Eugene Peterson, writing to a friend who, after a lifetime of struggle, finally begins to take hold of faith in Christ, says:

For both of us God has held the centre of our awareness and action. The contrast between your shaking your fist at Him and my shaking hands with Him may not be as significant as that it is God who has dominated both our lives… in your unbelieving (you) have probably thought about God more than I have in my believing.[2]

We should not, of course, be surprised. Luke, writing about Paul, makes it shockingly plain in Acts 17 that before we belong to the (wonderful and terrible) community of the redeemed in Christ, we belong even more fundamentally, along with every other man, woman and child, to the community of the created: 'we are God's offspring,' says verse 29. He is referring to all people, including the Greeks, Romans, Jews and Gentiles assembled for the meeting of the Areopagus in Athens, not just to followers of 'the Way'. I started to realize how often I behaved as if this were not the case, treating unbelievers as if they had nothing to offer and everything to receive, nothing to teach and everything to learn—and not at all with the respect and reverence due to someone fearfully, wonderfully and uniquely made by God.

I began to pray differently: 'Lord, what are you doing in N's life? Can I be alongside in some way, share the journey for a time…?' There is a sort of holiness to being in the presence of another, any other, just as there is in standing in creation and really noticing God's handiwork, lingering on details of colour and form, feeling the wind, smelling the earth and sea, hearing the bird and insect symphony, sad maybe that some of the instruments are already missing. The question is surely not 'How can I introduce Jesus?' but 'What is Jesus up to?' Again, Eugene Peterson, commenting on Mark 16:6–7, writes, 'In every visit, every meeting I attend, every appointment I keep, I have been anticipated. The risen Christ got there ahead of me… is in that room already. What is he doing? What is he saying? What is going on?'[3]

The problem is that, as Christians, we don't have a disembodied message to pass on: God didn't send an angel with a scroll; he sent his own Son. And now he sends us (John 20:21)—not the gospel as a box of chocolates, bunch of flowers, or even a cheque for a million pounds, but rather a message to live. In fact, we are the message, as Paul explained to the Corinthian church: 'You yourselves are our letter, written on our hearts, known and read by everybody' (2 Corinthians 3:2). D.L. Moody agreed with him, claiming that in any group of 100 people, only one will be reading the Bible, while 99 read the Christians. Unfortunately, as someone else pointed out, what we are speaks so loudly that people often can't hear a word we say anyway. And yet the good news is that because of God's indwelling Spirit, a process of transformation is taking place within the people of God so that what we truly are on the inside is becoming more and more Christ-like.

In our eagerness to pass on the gospel, we are inclined to forget how desperately we need to be receiving it ourselves. Followers of Jesus need forgiveness and filling with God's Spirit every bit as much as seekers after the truth. Remarkably, God has chosen to reveal what he is like not only through his prophets, his Son and his word, but also through his body, the Church. Many people in Western Europe at the beginning of the third millennium are familiar with what the gospel says, but what does it look like, feel like, and mean? What we really believe is revealed far more accurately through who we are than through what we say. It is etched in the quality of relationships formed, often painfully, within the pressures of frantic, busy lives. This is both the paradox and the power of Christian community.

So should we all leave our current situations and set up intentional Christian communities, so that the world can see more clearly what God is like? According to Acts 17:26, we are already set in specific communities by God himself. We do not need to create communities; rather, we need to identify and describe those we already belong to. The concept is not so much absent as in need of refining. Generally it is assumed that community means people of like mind or, at any rate, compatible values, choosing to live together. But we were to discover during the early years of A Rocha's life in Portugal that genuine community can be created with people of similar, different, or indeed no particular beliefs. It begins with inclusion; it involves love, acceptance and forgiveness; and it depends on a commitment to transparent relationships and self-giving hospitality, to a shared life of which the centrepiece is more often the kitchen table than the meeting room. Unconditional welcome is God's unreserved gift to us. We are not at liberty to introduce a different set of rules for those who arrive on our doorstep.

Herein lies the difference between evangelism and propaganda. Christian community is a risky undertaking. People are presented with the unedited version of our lives. All of us are works of art in progress, pots on the wheel; and, as with any artistic enterprise, we often seem to go backwards rather than forwards, creating more mess instead of the longed-for order. We are not predictable in our behaviour, especially in our goodness. 'Man is not an arithmetical expression,' wrote Dostoevsky, 'he is a mysterious and puzzling being, and his nature is extreme and contradictory all through.'[4] In *Surprised by Joy*, C.S. Lewis, peering inside himself and finding there 'a zoo of lusts, a bedlam of ambitions, a nursery of fears, a harem of fondled hatreds',[5] appears to reach an even more disturbing conclusion about the human condition. If such is the state of one person, what possible hope is there for realizing the psalmist's vision of harmony and blessing in Psalm 133, when several of these unpromising creatures are trying to live together?

The key to loving others and living peacefully together is surely to begin to take hold of how much we ourselves are already loved. Henri Nouwen, who struggled all his life to really experience this love for himself, nevertheless understood it well. He wrote, 'Long before your parents admired you or your friends acknowledged your gifts or your teacher, colleagues and employer encouraged you, you were already "chosen". The eyes of love had seen you as precious, as of infinite beauty, as of eternal value.'[6] This is a voice that has fallen silent, or perhaps never spoken, in too many people's lives. When we understand that we are loved, of unique significance and value, we become free to bow out of the ruthlessly competitive and comparative culture to which we belong, and offer the same forgiveness and acceptance to others that we have received.

The Archbishop of Canterbury, Dr Rowan Williams, in a recent address to the General Synod of the Church of England, said, 'God makes a difference of such a kind that a community appears, bound to and in his Son by the Spirit's power.' The apostle Peter's first letter to the scattered Christians instructs them to give hospitality to one another, and to use the gifts they have been given for the common good, but above all to 'love each other deeply'. Why? 'Because love covers over a multitude of sins' (1 Peter 4:8). There is a great deal to reflect on prayerfully in these passages, which speak to us of the reality of God's presence in his people. In surprising and visible ways, he can bring life to the world when we allow our relationships with him, each other and creation itself to be transformed.

❖

ENTERTAINING ANGELS IN COMMUNITY LIVING

Marcial Felgueiras, A Rocha Portugal

A chance encounter one cold and rainy February morning led to a life-changing event, the significance of which would only be realized years later. Helena, beautiful and tall, was a rising star in the modelling world. She modelled for some of the most famous fashion designers in the world and was frequently seen on the catwalks of Milan, Paris, Munich, New York and Tokyo. On this particular dreary February day, Helena had lost the confidence and glamour associated with the world of fashion and was instead a sad, weeping, broken shadow of her former self. Drenched by the rain and her own tears, she was the personification of despair. In the midst of Helena's desperation, a four-year-old girl called Lucy reached out and took Helena by the hand and invited her into the warmth and comfort of the A Rocha community at Cruzhina in Portugal. Lucy was unaware of the brokenness of her newfound friend but showed the Christ-like compassion of a child. She said to Helena, 'Don't worry! We are going to take good care of you.' In her childish innocence, Lucy echoed the words of the prophet Isaiah: 'Is it not to share your food with the hungry and to provide the poor wanderer with shelter' (Isaiah 58:7).

Helena stayed on in the A Rocha community for some time and found healing and restoration in the loving care of those around her. In the daily routines of the community, particularly the meal times, Helena discovered a new meaning to her life. She knew very little about birds and plants, but she did know about good food and was able to give her love through preparing delicious African meals. Helena's love of beauty was infectious and other people in the community began to appreciate the simple adoration she expressed towards such things as the sunsets. At Cruzhina, Helena learnt that she was important and was loved simply for herself and not for her outward appearance, money or influence.

Fifteen years later, Helena has left the fashion industry and completed a law degree. She is currently receiving training before working with a non-government organization as an international lawyer, focusing on human rights issues. Cruzhina, the birth place of A Rocha, has also moved on. The original team has left and the work of A Rocha has spread to many countries across the world.

A Rocha was never intended as a place of healing for hurt and broken people, and no one is trained in counselling, but God's grace, love and compassion are evident in the community. In community you need to live life with an open heart and an open door, always ready to be disturbed by the possibilities that God puts before you and the people that he brings through your door. Caring for God's world doesn't stop with the birds, plants, mammals and insects. In caring for God's creation in a loving community, there is always an acceptance of people, strangers and staff—a love and compassion that is infectious and results in healing for those that God sends, 'for by so doing some people have entertained angels without knowing it' (Hebrews 13:2).

INTEGRAL MISSION (ISAIAH 11:1–10)

Vinoth Ramachandra

The prophet Isaiah has announced the terrible news of the approach of the king of Assyria as Yahweh's agent of judgment on the southern kingdom of Judah (7:17–25), but now his gaze is lifted to a more expansive horizon. He sees Assyria itself defeated, and Yahweh's rule coming to the earth through a king on whom his Spirit rests, who brings not only deliverance for Israel but also salvation for the whole earth.

When Assyria was destroyed in 609BC, nothing emerged from its ruins. Not so with Israel. Out of the stump of the house of David will emerge a shoot (Isaiah 11:1). Nowhere in the book of Kings is any ruler described as the 'son of Jesse' except David himself (see 1 Samuel 20:27–33; 1 Kings 12:12–16). The shoot is not just another in David's house, but another David. More remarkably, he is also the root of Jesse (v. 10)—that which brought into being and supported the royal family into which he will be born. This is a paradox that awaits its resolution in the gospel message of the incarnate Son who is also the Messiah (compare Mark 12:35–37).

The Messiah's rule is marked by the following characteristics:

- *Delight in submission to God (vv. 2–3):* 'The fear of Yahweh' is a phrase that resonates throughout the Wisdom literature of Israel. It denotes not the cringing, servile fear that we show before powerful men who can hurt us, not the sheer terror we experience in the face of physical evil, and not even a generalized reverence towards the sacred and numinous, but rather an awed, grateful recognition of our absolute dependence on the Creator. In what must seem a paradox to modern ears, an ancient sage declares, 'The fear of the Lord is life indeed; filled with it one rests secure and suffers no harm' (Proverbs 19:23, NRSV). Wise leaders derive their wisdom from Yahweh, and wisdom issues in humility and justice (Proverbs 8:12–16). Leaders who have no time for listening to God's word end up either as tyrants (substituting themselves for God) or as weak and ineffective. Where the Holy Spirit fills a person, he or she delights to study God's word and to do his will in the world.

- *Justice for the poor (vv. 3b–5):* The leader who is filled with God's Spirit and has learned God's ways feels anger against every form of injustice and a compassion for the oppressed. The outpouring of the Holy Spirit leads to the practice of justice (compare Isaiah 32:15–16). Since Yahweh always champions the cause of the weak against the strong, the poor against the rich, in a society where there is no fear of God there will also be no concern for the poor.

  Instead of judging by appearance or listening to gossip (11:3b), Yahweh's anointed will rule with righteousness and faithfulness (v. 5). 'In place of the craven and petty house of David, or the arrogant and oppressive empire of Assyria, here is a king in whose hands the concerns of the weakest will be safe.'[1] These were the characteristics that the Israelite people saw in their God and longed for in their king. What Isaiah depicted in the Messiah was someone who would embody in a human way these features of Yahweh.

- *Ecological peace (vv. 6–9):* Human *shalom* and the *shalom* of the earth are intertwined. Greed and oppression fracture human solidarity. The resulting conflicts devastate the earth; so when the Messiah brings justice to the earth, this also marks the end to all violence against the earth and the animal creation. The kingdom of Yahweh is about the renewal of creation, the restoration of the peace that was lost because of human sin.

  The beautiful imagery of these verses portrays a world in which all fear, danger and violence have been banished. The most helpless and innocent can play with those who were formerly the most rapacious. The curse of Eden has been removed, and the enmity between the woman's seed and the serpent is gone (v. 8). This is the day that, in the words of the apostle Paul, the creation awaits 'in eager expectation' (Romans 8:19). Indeed, Paul's hope of a cosmic salvation is the best commentary on Isaiah's ancient prophecy: 'For the creation was subjected to frustration, not by its own choice, but by the will of the one who subjected it, in hope that the creation itself will be liberated from its bondage to decay and brought into the glorious freedom of the children of God' (Romans 8:20–21).

- *The earth filled with the knowledge of God (vv. 9b–10):* The transformed Eden is also Mount Zion, the place of revelation and of pilgrimage—a Zion that fills the whole earth. In every place, men and women enjoy peace, holiness and the knowledge of God to the fullest extent.

  Israel's calling will be fulfilled as the nations will come to know what Yahweh is like and worship him. Observe that it is the root of Jesse (that is, Jesus) who will be the focus of the people's search for God. It is he who fully reveals the heart of God to the world. It is not through their religions that men and women will find God, but through the coming of Jesus, the Messiah of God.

What a wonderful vision of *shalom*, God's plan for his entire creation! It summons us, as God's covenant people, to hold together what is often divorced in many contemporary evangelical circles, namely:

- To listen humbly to God's word.
- To promote social justice, locally and globally.
- To care for the earth and our non-human environment.
- To share the good news of Jesus among the nations.

Of these four interrelated areas of Christian discipleship, environmental concerns have not been a feature of mission education until relatively recently. At its Vancouver Assembly of 1983, the World Council of Churches rightly drew attention to the way the quest for economic justice, social peace and the 'integrity of creation' went hand in hand.[2] In recent years, nation states, or regions within states, have gone to war for control of petroleum supplies, diamonds and water. Excessive deforestation or over-grazing of cattle leads to soil erosion, which leads to the expansion of deserts, which leads to mass migrations, which leads to strain on the available resources of neighbouring countries to handle the influx of refugees—and this can, in turn, lead to war. The 'slash and burn' policies in the world's great forests (especially in Brazil and Indonesia) are due to pressures to grow cash crops and produce beef for export markets. In the long term, these destructive practices lead to permanent impoverishment of the soil and a worsening of rural poverty.

What does it mean to celebrate the goodness of the natural world and God's love for his creation, when many around us are gripped by apocalyptic images of nuclear, chemical and biological war, and when the only certainty appears to be that the earth, as well as humanity, has no future? While God himself respects the otherness of what he has made and delights in its creative diversity, we seem hell-bent on turning all animals and plants into mere consumer commodities, 'bio-machines' redesigned and shaped by genetic manipulation for the commercial profit of a few. Forests, water, seeds, the food chain, even the human genome itself are in danger of becoming commodities, representing the ultimate triumph of consumer society. When rich nations consign the notion of sustainable development to the scrap-heap, the biosphere is polluted, the land withers, and it is the poor who suffer the brunt of the fallout.

While every country has to deal with local problems of air and water pollution, there has been a growing recognition in recent years, among many scientists and environmental activists, that the massive ecological challenges facing the world require a coordinated global response. Foremost among these challenges are the escalation and proliferation of nuclear weapons technology; the threatened extinction of rainforests, which would also involve a massive loss of biodiversity; the threatened extinction of many animal species (tigers and some whale species being the most publicized); and the climatic changes, particularly global warming, brought about by the loss of forest cover and the profligate use of fossil fuels by the most industrialized nations of the world.

Understanding the problem and recommending solutions is one thing. Getting individuals and nations to repent of their profligate lifestyles for the sake of the global good is another. If global ecological problems such as global warming have any solutions, they can come only from a sense of human empathy and solidarity that might temper the short-sighted greed of purely commercial society. A white child born in New York, Paris or London will consume, pollute and waste more in his or her lifetime than 50 children born in a developing country, but it is these poor children who are the most likely to die from ensuing pollution and global warming. Christians, especially those in the rich nations and among the wealthier élites of poor nations, need to preach and demonstrate a gospel that has the power to liberate men and women from idolatry and greed, and to work with all who aspire for a more responsible use of the world's resources.

The horror of 11 September 2001 reminded us of our global interdependence. We now have a global alliance against terrorism—an alliance that is flawed and hypocritical, but nevertheless an alliance—but it is not enough to be against something. We also need to be for something. Why cannot we, as Christians, press for an alliance for global justice and a better global environment? Our interdependence makes it all the more necessary to undertake global collective action, and that must begin with us, the global body of Christ. But for us to think globally, rather than in narrowly partisan or ethnocentric ways, we must begin by recovering the biblical vision of *shalom*.

WORKING WITH VOLUNTEERS IN THE USA AND THE UK

Ginny Vroblesky and Dave Bookless,
A Rocha USA and A Rocha UK

'So… you're a *Christian* organization? Many of my relatives were killed by Christians.' The words hung in shocked silence in A Rocha UK's office. They were spoken by a Muslim volunteer from the former Yugoslavia, who had come as a refugee to Britain. She had heard of A Rocha from the local Voluntary Service Council and saw volunteering as a way of improving her English and using her skills. Thankfully, she had already got to know and like some of the team, and realized that our view on Christianity might be different from her past experience. By being accepted and valued as she was, some of her barriers and fears melted away and now she feels that she belongs with us.

In Anapolis, near Washington DC, A Rocha USA undertook a project called 'Listening to our Trees' to learn about the natural and cultural history of a neighbourhood by cataloguing and studying the trees within it. One of the volunteers who joined A Rocha USA in this project was a retired man, passionate about trees but initially suspicious of A Rocha's motivation. He confessed to a pretty negative experience of Christians: a church given some old woodland in trust that had sold it off for profit, and a Christian school that had ruthlessly exploited its property and destroyed historic trees. Through seeing A Rocha's genuine interest in nature, in places and local communities, he was forced to rethink his impression of Christians as greedy and deceptive. Moreover, through A Rocha USA's small-scale project, one man's lifelong wisdom and knowledge about his local environment has now been preserved in the form of a book on local trees, distributed throughout the community.

In A Rocha, we see 'mission' as starting with God, not people, and including everything that God calls his people to do in his world.

Narrower definitions have often led to treating people as simply 'targets for evangelism', and the natural world as irrelevant or even hostile. God's purposes are so much bigger. He not only created but actively sustains all things, and cares for all he has made—oceans, galaxies, wildlife and people—and calls us to steward and care with him. Our dealings with our fellow human beings, whether Christian or not, are set in the context of a God who cares in a holistic way, who provides food and shelter for his creatures, who is passionate about justice and right relationships with each other, as well as about restoring our broken relationships with God.

In A Rocha UK's urban London project, most of our volunteers do not have an active Christian faith. Some have social or physical disabilities. Some are asylum seekers, who are volunteering because they are not permitted to do paid work. One of our volunteers was a successful software engineer, disillusioned with his frantic work life, and decided to take a sabbatical from work. Before going travelling he volunteered with us and spent time helping with all kinds of menial and manual tasks. At the end, to our surprise, he was grateful. He was both moved and challenged by the example of the A Rocha community and the seamless way in which we join our work with the rest of our lives. He recognized that there was within the community a connection between people and the rest of God's creation, a sense of integration in contrast to the fragmented world in which he lived and worked.

Living in community—rather like living within an extended family—is often hard. We reveal the true selfishness of human nature, and volunteers bear witness to the good, the bad and the ugly! Nothing is hidden. In community everyone has to muck in, and volunteers see us taking turns in sharing all the menial tasks, like chopping salad and washing up. They join us in joking around, watching a film, and playing with the children in the community. Yet, time and again, our volunteers say that they love working here. Somehow, God shines through the busyness and the chaos. Why? Simply because we are ourselves, and people appreciate the acceptance and love they find. Nobody gets preached at, yet the witness of what people see and hear speaks more than words.

A NEW HEAVEN AND A NEW EARTH

Dave Bookless

Few biblical themes have excused environmental inaction more than this one. 'Why bother to care for the earth,' so the argument goes, 'if it will all be destroyed anyway?' This has not merely been the smug dismissal of a complacent few; it has at times been a policy source for the world's most powerful nation, influenced by block-voting from the Bible Belt. Yet, there is a one-word answer that holds true even should you choose to dismiss the rest of this chapter: obedience. If God commands us to care for the earth and its creatures responsibly (as every chapter in this book argues), we should do so from obedience, whether or not God should later choose to destroy them.

Having said that, there is an apparent tension between the earlier chapters of this book and the passages we are to look at here from Isaiah, 2 Peter and Revelation. The former emphasize all that is positive about God's world, whereas the latter are often taken as showing the destruction and replacement of that same creation. God is not inconsistent, however. He does not create in love, simply to destroy without reason. If we are to understand complex Bible passages full of vivid but potentially confusing imagery about 'new heavens and a new earth', we must do so within the context of the major themes that run from Genesis to Revelation. If the Bible is like a vast map of God's purposes, the major themes of creation, fall and redemption give us clear coordinates by which to locate ourselves. Only then can we get a true perspective on confusing details of the immediate scenery around us—on individual passages and verses. Without the wider picture, we can easily mistranslate, misinterpret and misapply. The context for studying Isaiah 65, Revelation 21 and 2 Peter 3 is to ask how they fit in with the overwhelmingly positive picture of creation given by the Bible as a whole—a picture of God's intimate involvement and ongoing care, and of our role as stewards, protectors and earth-keepers.

Isaiah 65:17–25 is the fullest of several Old Testament visions[1] of a future era of blessing for God's people in a new harmonious creation. It envisages an end to sorrow, pain and premature death (vv. 19–20), a time of self-sufficiency, prosperity and fulfilment (vv. 21–23), intimacy with God (v. 24) and ecological balance (v. 25). Some commentators have argued that this cannot be a literal vision, stressing that wolves, lions and serpents are biologically designed to be carnivorous predators. Others would see it as a radical re-making of the natural order, returning to the primeval paradise of Eden, a time before death in any form.

Either way, two things are clear. This is a very physical vision of the future—one where houses, vineyards and animals are material entities. There are no disembodied spirits strumming harps on ethereal clouds here. Secondly, it is an earthly vision; it is not about 'going to heaven' in some invisible parallel universe, but is about the earthing of heaven into creation. In talking of Jesus' teaching in the Gospels, Hans Küng says, 'God's Kingdom is creation healed', and that is very much the picture here. Creation is healed of human suffering and of conflict between animals, as God's kingly rule is re-established.

In Revelation 21:1–8, the theme of 'new heaven and a new earth' is revisited, with many parallels to the Isaiah passage but with Christ at the centre (vv. 6–8). From the perspective of environmental continuity, there is a worrying phrase at the end of verse 1, where we are told that the first earth and heaven 'had passed away, and there was no longer any sea'. Does this mean the annihilation of the present planet earth, and its replacement by a new improved model? Quite simply, no—for three reasons.

First, as the New Bible Commentary states, 'the description may be purely poetic to enhance the terrifying grandeur of the scene'.[2] The surrounding chapters show that we are dealing with symbolic, apocalyptic language. In Revelation 20:11 we find earth and heaven fleeing from God's presence, and yet shortly afterwards (v. 13) the sea disgorges the dead that were in it, despite the sea's presumably being part of the earth that had run away! Again, in chapter 22 the river of life is central to the imagery— and rivers tend to flow into seas. The emphasis of the symbolic language is not on destroying the old, but on 'making everything new' (21:5) as God comes down from heaven, removing sin and chaos (the sea being a common Old Testament metaphor for the forces of chaos), and makes his home with humanity.

Second, there are clear links in Revelation 20—22 not only with the new earth of Isaiah 65, but also with the first creation of Genesis 1—2. Michael Wilcock's commentary, *The Message of Revelation*, says, 'The most significant parallel is with the opening chapters of Genesis. This tie-rod, running from end to end of the sixty-six books, shows that the third revelation of heaven here... is a summary of the biblical doctrine of creation.'[3] Similarly, John Sweet describes the picture as one of 'paradise regained',[4] marking parallels between the river of Genesis 2:10 and that of Revelation 22:1; the tree of life (Genesis 2:9), made inaccessible through expulsion from Eden, now yielding healing and fruitfulness (Revelation 22:2); and the curse on people and the earth, with the removal of God's intimate presence (Genesis 3:16–24), giving way to blessing and renewed intimacy (Revelation 21:3–4; 22:3–5). Underlying all these parallels is the implication of a continuous link between the 'old' and 'new' earth and heaven. Richard Bauckham rightfully reminds us that understanding God as Creator was central to how Jews and Christians understood the future of the earth: 'If God was the transcendent source of all things, he could also be the source of quite new possibilities for his creation in the future.'[5]

Third, and critically, 'new' in this context need not mean brand new, but renewed. New Testament Greek, unlike English, has two words for new, *neos* meaning totally (or existentially) new, and *kainos* meaning 'new as to form or quality'.[6] The Bible consistently uses *kainos* for the 'new' creation. Whether it is the 'new Jerusalem' (Revelation 3:12; 21:2), the 'new heavens and new earth' (Revelation 21:1; 2 Peter 3:13), or God saying 'I am making everything new!' (Revelation 21:5), the word is consistently *kainos*: renewed rather than new. We are used to this meaning of 'new' in other contexts: 2 Corinthians 5:17 says, 'If anyone is in Christ, he is a new creation; the old has gone, the new has come!'[7] A Christian is a new creation in a very real sense, but retains their 'old' physical body. So also the new creation will be radically transformed, healed and cleansed of sin and evil, but will have a fundamental continuity with the present creation. In the same way that God recycles broken, scarred, twisted human beings into new creations in Christ, so the 'old' earth will be recycled into God's new creation, where 'the kingdom of the world has become the kingdom of our Lord and of his Christ, and he will reign for ever and ever' (Revelation 11:15).

Finally we come to 2 Peter 3:3–13, perhaps the passage above all others that has led to confusion about the destiny of the planet. Poor English translations bear much responsibility here. In the 17th-century King James Version, often followed by later versions, we read of the heavens and earth being 'reserved unto fire against the day of judgment' (v. 7), the heavens passing away, the elements melting and the earth being 'burned up' (v. 10), and finally an implied replacement by 'new heavens and a new earth' (v. 13). Game, set and match to the 'turn or burn' brigade? Not at all! At every point, if we examine the text in its context, we see that the passage is actually about decisive cleansing judgment, where evil is destroyed and God's creation purified. In verses 5–7, the parallel with Noah's flood is a key to understanding this. The flood that 'deluged and destroyed' the world (v. 6) is compared with the final judgment; yet, of course, the earth was not totally destroyed in the flood. Noah's family and representatives of every living species were saved to live again on the same earth. The picture is of selective judgment, not complete destruction. Just as the water of the flood cleansed the earth, so the refiner's fire[8] of verse 7 will purify the world from evil, but not annihilate it.[9]

2 Peter 3:10 and 12 talk further about the fire of judgment, but also suffer from poor translation. The 'elements' that are destroyed are not those of the periodic table, from which the earth is constructed; they are the elemental forces of the universe, the distorted powers that have thwarted God's rule on earth.[10] So the earth, finally, is not 'burned up' (v. 10, KJV), but 'laid bare' (NIV, NEB) or 'disclosed' (NRSV)—a word with connotations of rediscovery and revelation.[11] Thus we can agree with R.J. Berry that 'even such verses as 2 Peter 3:10 need not be interpreted to mean the end of this present creation—particularly since the context emphasizes the scrutiny of human deeds rather than annihilation'.[12] Finally, this makes sense of verse 13, where the 'new heaven and... new earth, the home of righteousness' are new in character, quality and purity, but also in continuance with God's original creation.

In conclusion, these key passages teach us central truths about the future of the earth, and enable us to contribute fruitfully to the environmental debate. On the one hand, Christians do not accept worldviews which teach that 'things can only get better'—that people and the planet itself are evolving into a gradually higher and improved plane of existence. This idea goes against the evidence of rapidly increasing ecological disaster and against biblical teaching of a cataclysmic cosmic judgment, when much will be destroyed. On the other hand, Christians need not accept the pessimism that infects the environmental movement today, as few seem ready to change their lifestyles. Although the Bible teaches judgment, it is that of a loving and holy God who wishes to restore and redeem all that has gone wrong, and with whom there is hope for the planet. Rather than an otherworldly hope of 'pie in the sky when you die', the Bible offers a tangible, harmonious, restored creation—God's kingdom, 'on earth as it is in heaven'. Creation's groaning for 'liberation' from its 'bondage to decay' is fulfilled: through its labour pains, a new creation is birthed (Romans 8:19–22), and 'all things, whether things on earth or things in heaven' are reconciled to God in Christ (Colossians 1:19–20). Finally, every creature in earth and heaven and sea can sing God's praise together: 'To him who sits on the throne and to the Lamb be praise and honour and glory and power, for ever and ever!' (Revelation 5:13). What a vision to cause us to worship, not only in words but in our actions and in our lifestyle decisions!

HINTS OF GLORY AROUND THE WORLD

Peter and Miranda Harris, A Rocha International

Jesus' life on earth, as he brought in the kingdom of God, was lived out in a specific time and place, among human communities and in a particular local environment. It was a place in God's creation that he knew well. His life and message made a local difference. The difference was sometimes dramatic and was often experienced in the context of the material world, through such things as food and drink, or through the weather and livestock.

The continuing presence of the marshes at Alvor in Portugal and Aammiq in Lebanon, and the landscape at Minet in Southall, UK, show that the gospel can indeed make a difference to the well-being of the physical world. To watch migrating waders feeding at dusk on the salt pans or mudflats at Alvor, or to see pools and trees in Southall where once the land was sterile and rubbish-strewn, is to witness a kind of miracle.

Christian health professionals have long been used to experiencing this kind of healing change in the results of their own work on the human body, but we have been slow to see the implications of the gospel for the wider non-human creation. There remain many challenges as this biblical imperative takes hold of the heart and mind of the Church around the world.

At this time and in many different locations around the world, creation groans in anticipation of a Christian response to the care of God's creation. There are many questions that loom large for A Rocha. Can we hope that the remaining fragments of coastal forest around Watamu might be preserved through the work of A Rocha Kenya? Will the Vallée des Baux in France look different in ten years' time as a result of A Rocha France's work with local landowners? Will there be some help for the extremely threatened bird populations of the Czech Republic, as Pavel and Radka and their team apply the fruits of their research and education work more widely? What hope is there for the increasingly bare slopes of the Kalrayan Hills in western India? Can we respond to the current requests for help from Brazil, Mali, Guinea and many other countries where people are seeing whole ecosystems and habitats disappearing almost as they watch? Can the current indifference to the plight of creation, which is all too common in the considerable Christian communities of wealthier Western countries, be turned to repentance and renewal of life? Can the questions of belief that drive environmental change around the world be discussed more openly by the very diverse groups who are now achieving so much for the protection of biodiversity?

Christians have much to learn from the impressive array of answers that these people and groups can give to questions that address the technical side of their work, but we urgently need to remember that they are often preceded by vital 'why' questions, if we are truly to learn from each other and find sustainable solutions.

Probably the one distinctive that marks out Christians from others who work for a whole environment is hope. The biblical gospel is given to see creation healed here and now as we wait for the final and promised redemption in Christ. If we are to catch a glimpse of what that will mean, we need to see its partial and imperfect reflection in local transformation of personal lives, human society, and the creation around us.

We are all called to follow in the steps of a creator who cares. We can give practical expression to his caring and his concerns in the places and times where we live, following the pattern of his fully obedient Son, who promises his presence and the power of his Spirit, for wisdom, for real and lasting change.

FURTHER READING

J. Moltmann, *Theology of Hope* (SCM Press, 1967)
J. Moltmann, *God in Creation* (SCM Press, 1985)
Wim Rietkerk, *The Future Great Planet Earth* (Good Books, Mussoorie, India)
N.T. Wright, *New Heavens, New Earth* (Grove Books, 1999)

QUESTIONS FOR GROUP DISCUSSION

CHAPTER 1

1. How does Isaiah help us to understand the relevance of God's creation work in our own context?
2. Where do you see hurry and/or procrastination desecrating the gift of time in your own life?
3. What role does the Sabbath play in God's creation work and in your own rhythms of life?
4. How does worship help us to participate in God's work?
5. Where do you see the Spirit of God moving over chaos and mess in your own daily living?

CHAPTER 2

1. In what ways could Adam and Eve be said to be the first scientists?
2. Can you think of parallels between the pursuit of science and the pursuit of faith? Can you think also of differences?
3. In which areas of scientific research do you think it is particularly appropriate for Christians to get involved?
4. What examples of technology can you think of that truly serve humanity and creation?
5. How is God revealed in (a) his creation and (b) his word, and how do people respond to these two 'books' today?

CHAPTER 3

1. How and why does our relationship with God affect our relationships with others, with ourselves, and with the rest of creation?
2. In what ways does *Homo divinus* differ in nature and behaviour from *Homo sapiens*?

3. Does nature have 'rights'?
4. How do Christian motives for environmental protection and repair differ from those of others?
5. Is Lynn White's criticism of the Christian attitude to creation correct? How can this be redressed?

CHAPTER 4

1. How has our reading of the Genesis passages affected our ideas about creation care?
2. What does the Noah story say about the human role in God's plan for the redemption of creation?
3. How can our faith and technology be put to the service of all creation?
4. How do we understand our covenant relationship with God today?
5. What are some of the ways in which the Church can lead the way in caring for creation?

CHAPTER 5

1. What kind of measures today would encourage an approach to poverty that maximizes the social participation of the poor within the community?
2. What are the social and spiritual effects of prolonged debt in society?
3. How can we ensure that the theological dimensions of the jubilee are included in whatever social or economic programmes we develop for the relief of poverty and care of creation?
4. How would you answer the opinion that, because the Old Testament's concern with the land is seen as fulfilled in Christ, Christians need have no interest in the earth or its future?
5. How might our use of the jubilee model today both liberate the oppressed and influence the transformation of nature?

CHAPTER 6

1. What is wisdom's role in creation?
2. What are your plans for success? Is God's will the basis of your plans or an afterthought?
3. From God's conversation with Job, how do we understand the place of humanity in his creation?
4. Think of the richest and the poorest people you know. Have stereotypes about wealth and poverty affected your attitude towards them?
5. What does biblical wisdom have to say to the problem of unbelief?

CHAPTER 7

1. What are the 'earth' or 'environment' aspects of the account of Jesus walking with his disciples in the grain fields?
2. What connections with other biblical texts or themes do you notice?
3. What does the story tell you about Jesus' relationship with the earth, and what lessons are there for us?
4. How might sharing, caring and restraint be principles for change in the context of farming and food production, and what effect would they have on your community?
5. In God's economy there are enough resources to sustain his world— discuss!

CHAPTER 8

1. Why might life feel shallow or even empty without a sense of transcendence?
2. Have you ever questioned the reality of 'Nature'? How does this chapter help you to critique the concept?
3. Define the significance of including the incarnation within the biblical revelation of creation.
4. Why might theism be the only theory of the universe that could really explain its existence?
5. What are the dangers of splitting off science from religion?

CHAPTER 9

1. How central is the resurrection to your understanding of Christian faith?
2. In what ways did Jesus' resurrection impact the lives of the first Christians?
3. What implications does Jesus' resurrection have for the future of the material created world?
4. What is the relationship between suffering and resurrection for the Christian?
5. How can we practise resurrection in today's world?

CHAPTER 10

1. What might be wrong with a privatized, independent faith?
2. How easy is it to recognize God at work in the life of others?
3. How do you respond to the idea of being God's living message?
4. Why is it hard to love others and live peacefully together without first experiencing God's love for us?
5. What are the challenges for a Christian community regarding unity and diversity?

CHAPTER 11

1. Which element of Isaiah's prophecy do you find most encouraging? Why?
2. How much do environmental concerns feature in your understanding of *shalom*?
3. What part can individual Christians play in responding to the ecological challenges facing our world?
4. What might 'thinking and acting globally' mean in practice?
5. Before you can promote economic and social justice both locally and globally, what lifestyle changes might you need to make yourself?

CHAPTER 12

1. What difference does it make whether the present creation is replaced by God or renewed by him?
2. How physical is your concept of life in 'the new heavens and the new earth'?
3. How central is your understanding of God as creator to your hope for the future of the earth?
4. How might the biblical truths about the future of the earth contribute to the environmental debate today?
5. Can you see something of the renewed creation in the world today?

NOTES

Introduction

1 Mark Noll, *The Scandal of the Evangelical Mind* (Eerdmans, 1994).
2 The Declaration was issued in 1994 and asserts that the earth belongs to God and that we are responsible to him for it. It sets out five Christian affirmations relevant to discernible violations of creation, identifies four spiritual responses, and then calls upon Christians to seek to apply these responses in specified ways. See R.J. Berry (ed.), *The Care of Creation* (IVP, 2000).

Chapter 2: God and the image bearers

1 The books in the 'Further reading' section of this chapter all expound the idea of humans in the image of God. See p. 38.
2 For example, Lynn White, *Science* 155 (1967), pp. 1203–07.
3 C.S. Lewis, *Reflections on the Psalms* (Fontana, 1961), p. 56.
4 C.H. Spurgeon, *Treasury of David* (Hendrickson, 1988).

Chapter 3: Rejection of the creator

1 C.E.B. Cranfield, 'Some observations on Romans 8:19–21', in R. Banks (ed.), *Reconciliation and Hope: New Testament Essays on Atonement and Eschatology* (Eerdmans, 1974), pp. 224–30.
2 D. Kidner, *Genesis: An Introduction and Commentary* (IVP, 1967), p. 73.
3 H. Blocher, *In the Beginning* (IVP, 1984), p. 158.

Chapter 4: God's covenant with the earth

1 See Isaiah, Ezekiel and Hosea.
2 *2000 IUCN Red List of Threatened Species* compiled by Craig Hilton Taylor (IUCN, 2000), www.iucn.org.
3 Bruce K. Waltke, *Genesis* (Zondervan, 2001).

4   William F. May, 'Four Mischievous Theories of Sex', in A Klass and L. Klass (eds), *Wing to Wing, Oar to Oar* (University of Notre Dame Press, 2000).
5   See Hosea's predictions of marine devastation in 4:1–3, which have only come about in recent decades.
6   'Gospel and Creation' tapes and CDs available from A Rocha, www.arocha.org.
7   Even in a national context, it can be striking to see how significant a part the church can play, as in the UK, for example, where the Church of England is one of the major landowners.

Chapter 5: Sabbath for the land and jubilee

1   Quoted in Hans Ucko (ed.), *Jubilee Challenge: Utopia or Possibility* (WCC Publications, 1997), p. 109.
2   For a fuller explanation of these hermeneutical methods, see C.J.H. Wright, *Old Testament Ethics for the People of God* (IVP, 2004), chapters 3 and 6.
3   Some creative applications are found in John Mason, 'Assisting the Poor', *Transformation* 4.2 (1987), and Stephen Charles Mott, 'Economic Thought', *Transformation* 4.3–4 (1987).
4   Wright, *Old Testament Ethics for the People of God*, p. 209.

Chapter 7: Creation and the Gospels

1   A. Edersheim, *The Life and Times of Jesus the Messiah* (Hendrickson, 1883, republished 1993).
2   The Old Testament economy, in general, shows a special concern for the vulnerable and the poor. Laws of tithing (Deuteronomy 14:28–29) and gleaning (Deuteronomy 24:19–22), for example, make provision for those without assets, protection, power or standing ground in the community (strangers, widows and orphans). Indeed, Deuteronomy 14:29 implies that the success of future harvests depends on sharing with, and caring for, the poor and needy.
3   This principle of restraint, on the use of land, livestock and labour, on the concentration of wealth, and on expansionism, can be discerned in many biblical themes and writings, in addition to the Sabbath

and jubilee provisions. For example, the taking of interest on loans was prohibited between Israelites (Exodus 22:25; Leviticus 25:36; Deuteronomy 23:19); there was strict control on what could be taken as pledges in security for loans and how (Exodus 22:26; Deuteronomy 24:6, 10); and the moving of boundary stones that marked out family land was strictly proscribed (Deuteronomy 19:14).

4   Luke 6:1 (AV) states that the Sabbath was the 'second after the first', which Edersheim argued as referring either to the first or the second Sabbath after the second day of Passover. The barley harvest was inaugurated by the feast of Firstfruits, shortly after Passover. The wheat harvest came later, at Pentecost.

5   A conservative estimate by researchers at Essex University of the external environmental and health costs of farming in the UK put the bill at around £2 billion per year. A comparable figure for the US is £13 billion (John R. Pretty, *Agri-culture: Reconnecting People, Land and Nature* [Earthscan, 2002]).

6   C. Jones and S.P. Carruthers, *Corporate Power, People and the Land*, www.agriculture-theology.org.uk/articles/CorporatePowerPeopleLand.htm.

7   W. Brueggemann, *The Land* (Fortress Press, 1977). It is noteworthy that the relaxation of Sunday trading laws has impacted most on those on the lowest incomes, such as those working at checkout counters in DIY superstores or stacking shelves in supermarkets.

8   J. Moltmann, *God in Creation: An Ecological Doctrine of Creation* (SCM Press, 1985).

9   J. Jones, *Jesus and the Earth* (SPCK, 2003), p. 35.

10 E.P Echlin, *The Cosmic Circle* (The Columba Press, 2004).

11 Echlin, *The Cosmic Circle*, p. 76.

12 Jones, *Jesus and the Earth*.

13 Echlin, *The Cosmic Circle*.

14 Fra Angelico (Guido di Pietro), *Noli me tangere* (1440–41), Convent of San Marco, Florence.

15 Quoted in I. Bradley, *God is Green* (DLT, 1990).

16 Michelangelo Merisi da Caravaggio, *Supper at Emmaus* (1601–2), National Gallery, London.

17 Echlin, *The Cosmic Circle*, p. 98.

Chapter Eight: Creation and incarnation

1 Loren Eisley, 'The Cosmic Orphan', in *Encylopaedia Britannica* (Propaedia, 1974), pp. 206–8.

2 William Temple, *Religious Experience, and other Essays and Addresses*, ed. Canon E. Baker (James Clarke & Co, 1959), p. 161.

3 Matthew Fox, 'Creation-Centred Spirituality', in Gordon Wakefield, *Dictionary of Christian Spirituality* (SCM Press, 1983), p. 99.

4 Rosemary Radford Ruether, *Sexism and God-Talk: towards a Feminist Theology* (Prudence Press, 1983), p. 77.

5 Lynn White, 'The historical roots of our ecological crisis', *Science 155*, pp. 1203–07.

6 Sallie McFague, *Models of God: Theology for an Ecological Nuclear Age* (Fortress Press, 1987), pp. 69–78.

7 Prudence Allen, *Concept of Woman Vol. 1: The Aristotelian Revolution* (Eerdmans, 1997).

8 Robert Boyle, 'A Critique of Nature Vulgarly So-Called', in Richard Baulton (ed.), *Theological Works* (W. Taylor, 1715).

9 Ernest Becker, *The Denial of Death* (The Freepress, 1973), p. 56.

10 Paisley Livingston, *Models of Desire: Rene Girard and the Psychology of Mimesis* (The Johns Hopkins University Press, 1992), pp. xii–xiii, 1, 4.

11 James G. Williams (ed.), *The Girard Reader* (Crossroad, 1996), p. 33.

12 Sebastian Moore, *The Inner Loneliness* (Crossroad, 1982), p. 9.

13 Rowan Williams, *On Christian Theology* (Blackwell, 2000), p. 74.

14 Stanley L. Jaki, *Cosmos and Creation* (Scottish Academic Press, 1980).

15 T.F. Torrance, *Theology in Reconciliation* (Geoffrey Chapman, 1975), pp. 31–39.

16 T.F. Torrance, *Divine Meaning: Studies in Patristic Hermeneutics* (T&T Clark, 1995), pp. 230, 385.

17 T.F. Torrance, *The Trinitarian Faith* (T&T Clark, 1988), p. 51.

18 Tapio Luoma, *Incarnation and Physics: Natural Science in the Theology of T.F. Torrance* (Oxford University Press, 2002)

19 T.F. Torrance, *Christian Theology and Scientific Culture* (Christian Journals Ltd., 1980), p. 127.

20 Torrance, *Christian Theology*, p. 128.

21 Jurgen Moltmann, *God and Creation* (Fortress Press, 1993)

22 Moltmann, *God and Creation*, p. 11.

23 Moltmann, *God and Creation*, p. 211.

24 Jurgen Moltmann, *The Way of Jesus Christ* (Fortress Press, 1993), p. 294.

25 Moltmann, *The Way of Jesus Christ*, p. 296.

26 See the excellent critique of Richard Bauckham, *The Theology of Jurgen Moltmann* (T&T Clark, 1995), pp. 183–98.

27 Colin Gunton, *Enlightenment and Alienation: An Essay towards a Trinitarian Theology* (Marshall, Morgan & Scott, 1985), p. 141.

28 Colin Gunton, *The One, the Three and the Many: God, Creation and the Culture of Modernity* (Cambridge University Press, 1993), pp. 46–51.

29 Gunton, *The One, the Three and the Many*, p. 149.

30 Gunton, *The One, the Three and the Many*, p. 153.

31 Colin Gunton, *The Triune Creator: A Historical and Systematic Study* (Edinburgh University Press, 1998), p. 223.

32 Bruce Walkte, *Genesis* (Zondervan, 2001), p. 71.

33 James M. Houston, *I Believe in the Creator* (Eerdmans, 1980).

34 A.J. Heschel, *The Sabbath: Its Meaning for Modern Man* (Farrar, Strauss & Giroux, 1986), p. 6.

35 John Calvin, *Institutes* 2.8.29.

36 John Calvin, *Commentary on Hebrews* 4.10.

Chapter 9: Jesus and the resurrection

1 Reason became the goddess of the mind because of the assumption, which Descartes had already proposed, that mathematics is the most certain form of knowledge. '"Noumenal" or intuitive knowledge is considered a much less trustworthy form of knowing than "phenomenal" or objective knowledge'. James Houston, *The Heart's Desire: A Guide to Personal Fulfilment* (Lion, 1992), p. 100.

2 James Alison, *Knowing Jesus* (SPCK, 1998), p. 6.

3 Alison, *Knowing Jesus*, p. 12.

4 Alison, *Knowing Jesus*, p. 10.

5 When Luke says that Jesus interpreted the Bible, he doesn't mean that Jesus collected a few, or even a few dozen, isolated texts, verses chosen at random. He means the whole story from Genesis to Chronicles pointed towards the fulfilment which could only be found when God's anointed took Israel's suffering, and hence the world's suffering, onto himself. Tom Wright, *Luke for Everyone* (SPCK, 2001), p. 294.

6 Alison, *Knowing Jesus*, p. 17.

7   N.T. Wright, *The Resurrection of the Son of God* (SPCK, 2003).
8   Wendell Berry, 'Manifesto: The Mad Farmer Liberation Front' (www.ecobooks.com).

Chapter 10: Community and our inheritance

1   Jean Vanier, *Becoming Human* (The Canadian Broadcasting Corporation, 1998).
2   Eugene Peterson, *The Wisdom of Each Other* (Zondervan, 1998).
3   Eugene Peterson, *Under the Unpredictable Plant* (Eerdmans, 1992).
4   Quoted by Nicholas Berdyaev in *Dostoyevsky* (Living Age Books, 1957), p. 53.
5   C.S. Lewis, *Surprised by Joy* (Fount, 2002), p. 226.
6   Henri Nouwen, *Life of the Beloved* (Hodder & Stoughton, 2002).

Chapter 11: Integral mission (Isaiah 11:1–10)

1   John N. Oswalt, *The Book of Isaiah: Chapters 1—39*, NICOT (Eerdmans, 1986), p. 277.
2   *Gathered for Life* (WCC Publications, 1983).

Chapter 12: A new heaven and a new earth

1   For example, Isaiah 11:6–9; Hosea 2:18.
2   *New Bible Commentary* (3rd edn) (IVP, 1970), p. 1306.
3   M. Wilcock, *The Message of Revelation: I Saw Heaven Opened* (IVP, 1975), p. 212.
4   J. Sweet, *Revelation* (SCM Press, 1979), p. 311.
5   R. Bauckham, *The Theology of the Book of Revelation* (Cambridge University Press, 1993), p. 48.
6   W.E. Vine, *Expository Dictionary of Bible Words* (Marshall, Morgan & Scott, 1981), p. 109.
7   As well as 2 Corinthians 5:17, see this use of *kainos* for 'new' in, for example, Galatians 6:15; Ephesians 2:15; 4:24.
8   Malachi 3:2–3: the 'day of the Lord' was a familiar Jewish phrase for the final judgment, seen as fire that refined without destroying completely.

9   The Good News Bible's use of 'destroyed' in 2 Peter 3:7 is supported neither by the Greek text nor other translations—a classic case of translators reading their own prejudices into the Bible!

10 The Greek for 'elements' is *stoicheia*, as also in Galatians 4:3, 9 and Colossians 2:8, 20 ('basic principles' which we were formerly enslaved to).

11 The Greek word *heuretesetai*, meaning 'found, made clear or disclosed' is found in the most reliable ancient New Testament Greek texts, including Codex Siniaticus and Codex Vaticanus. It is possible that the alternative 'burned up', found in a few corrupted texts, may have been influenced by pagan Gnostic thought, which saw matter as inferior to spirit.

12 R.J. Berry (ed.), *The Care of Creation* (IVP, 2000), p. 181.